MW00443696

Cover and forward Copyright © 2022 by Tom Kelchner

ISBN: 978-1-7345955-0-5

1. COOKING / Regional & Ethnic / American / Southern States
2. COOKING / Specific Ingredients / Seafood

Tom Kelchner also is the author of:

To Great Grandmother's House We Go; American Comfort Food from the 1970s, 60s and before

Chicamacomico Cookery
Facsimile Edition

Tom Kelchner

Forward to the Chicamacomico Cookery facsimile edition

This is much more than a reprint of a 1960s volunteer fire company charity cookbook. This is the record of an effort to support a life-saving organization in an North Carolina Outer Banks community with a heritage of spectacular heroism.

Today the Chicamacomico Banks Volunteer Fire Department in Rodanthe, North Carolina, is still providing heroic rescues routinely, largely for tourists who get swept into deep water by rip tides or fall victim to medical emergencies. There also are (very rare) shark attacks. Rip tides, heart attacks and shark attacks are sometimes fatal, so, there is nothing routine about the volunteers' "routine."

In the backs of the minds of the volunteers must be the image of the spectacular 1918 rescue of the British crew from a burning tanker, HMS Mirlo, that had been torpedoed by a German submarine seven miles off shore. Captain John Allen Midgett, head of the Chicamacomico Life Saving Station, and his crew struggled through rough seas to rescue the men -- six from an overturned lifeboat in a sea of flaming fuel. They then helped the 42 survivors of the action to safety.

In 1921, the British government awarded Gold Lifesaving Medals for "Gallantry and Humanity in Saving Life at sea" to the rescuers. The incident is accepted as the most spectacular rescue in Life-Saving Service/Coast Guard history.

The North Carolina Outer Banks is a wonderful and unique place. The people who have lived on those barrier islands for more than 300 years sometimes struggled to find enough to eat, but they have always used their ingenuity to turn the wonderful fish, game and other foods available to them into great meals.

Sometime between 1963 and 1974, the Ladies Auxiliary of the Chicamacomico Banks Volunteer Fire Department of Rodanthe rounded up 197 recipes, many unique to their families and the Outer Banks, and published a fund-raising cookbook. This facsimile edition is an attempt to preserve those recipes and honor the 55 contributors -- many descendants of the HMS Mirlo rescuers.

Nothing is known of the book's history. We only know it was published after 1963 -- since there are Zip codes in some advertisements – and before 1974, because one of the listed contributors, Bernice Ballance of Buxton, died that year at the age of 89.[1] "Captain" Ballance was well known on the Outer Banks for holding the record catch of a 75-pound channel bass which he landed in the 1920s. The record stood for nearly 20 years.[2]

The copy we used for this facsimile edition surfaced in Michigan when a friend's mother downsized her cookbook collection. She said she did not remember where she got it, probably at a library used-book sale.

Charity and community cookbooks, abbreviated CCB's by some scholars, had their beginning in 1864. That year a women's group in Philadelphia published *A Poetical Cook-Book* to raise money for a "sanitary fair" to aid soldiers fighting in the Civil War. It was an idea that caught on. Between then and the start of the First World War, 5,000 of them were published, chiefly by women's groups. The projects gave women the opportunity to learn organizational skills that they would use in many other endeavors, including the efforts to gain women the vote, fund charity organizations and support the prohibitionist movement. Food scholars regard the books as a vast untapped resource for the study of recipes and women's history.[3]

In reality, what one finds in charity cookbooks are the recipes that were circulating in newspapers and magazines of their day. In older CCBs those can be interesting, but one can only use so many recipes for Jell-O, cheese and macaroni and "American" goulash. It is certain, though, that each one also contains at least a few priceless gems: family and local recipes that have been handed down through the generations. In many cases, these fund-raiser cookbooks are the only place those recipes exist outside the family recipe boxes and the notebooks that vanish as the generations roll on.

Hopefully this facsimile edition will keep alive the recipes and the memory of some of the heroic people of the North Carolina Outer Banks.

1. "Other Deaths," *News and Observer*, Raleigh, North Carolina, Mar. 22, 1974, pp 31
2. "Big Game Fish Hitting off Carolina Coast," *Charlotte Observer*, Charlotte, North Carolina, May 14, 1971, pp 69
3. Smith, Ed., *The Oxford Encyclopedia of Food and Drink in America,* (New York: Oxford University Press, 2004), pp 291

CHICAMACOMICO COOKERY

CHICAMACOMICO COAST GUARD STATION

CHICAMACOMICO
BANKS VOLUNTEER FIRE DEPARTMENT
– LADIES AUXILIARY –

Rodanthe – Waves, North Carolina

MEMBERS AND SPONSORS

President . . . . Mrs. A. H. Gray, Jr.

Vice-President . . . . Mrs. Alexander Meekins

Secretary . . . . Mrs. Lansdell Anderson

Treasurer . . . . Mrs. Dalton Hooper

Mrs. Woodrow Edwards
Mrs. A. H. Gray
Mrs. Julian Gray
Mrs. Rudy Gray
Mrs. Johnny Hooper
Mrs. Burgess Hooper
Mrs. John Herbert
Mrs. Jethro Midgett
Mrs. Camille Midgett
Mrs. Leland Midgett
Mrs. Ersie Midgett
Mrs. Levine Midgett
Mrs. Sarah Midgett
Mrs. Dewey Midgett
Mrs. Louis Midgett
Mrs. Lurania Midgett
Mrs. Carethia Midgett
Mrs. Cedric Midgett
Mrs. Herbert Midgett
Mrs. Mildred Midgett
Mrs. Odessa Midgett
Mrs. Colenda Midgett

Mrs. Sara Midgett
Mrs. Sudie Payne
Mrs. Ethel O'Neal
Mrs. Virginia O'Neal
Mrs. Rose-Ann O'Neal
Mrs. Maggie Smith
Mrs. Marvin Toler
Mrs. Patsy Rollinson
Mr. & Mrs. Karl Kuhlmann
Mr. & Mrs. Cecil Midgett
Mr & Mrs. Ed. T. Gentry
Mrs. Rose B. Young
Mr. & Mrs. Jerry Holloman
Mr. & Mrs. Rudy Gray
Mr. & Mrs. Charles Williams
Capt. & Mrs. Bernice Ballance
Mr. & Mrs. Asa H. Gray, Jr.
Mr & Mrs. C. A. Midgett
Capt. & Mrs. Dudley Burrus
Mr. & Mrs. Oscar O'Neal
Mr. & Mrs. Dalton Hooper

CHICAMACOMICO BANKS

Where is this area - or where was it? From whence came this name of lore and yore? Author David Stick's interesting book, "The Outer Banks of North Carolina", presents the answers.

But first, how does one pronounce this derivitive of a native Indian name? It's easy! Chic-a-ma--com-i-co. Accent "Chic" moderately, then pronounce each "a" in "a-ma" as in "ah" -- low-key and long. Then really stress your accent on "com" and wind up with a fast but low-key "i-co". Chic-a-ma-COM--i-co. First, say it real slow. Repeat it, and then say it at normal speed, hitting that "COM" hard and the "i-co" fast. You'll never forget it!

The name first appeared in an official record of 1730. It was described as a 20--mile stretch of Hatteras Island from an inlet, now nonexistent but which then crossed the Pea Island Refuge, southward to Little Kinnakeet where you now see an old Lifesaving Station on the way down to Buxton. Actually, some pioneers had settled here nearly 30 years earlier.

Long before the Civil War, the live oak and cedar forests then here became highly desired timber for the famous clipper ships, so sand dunes gradually replaced the woodlands, and fishing became the primary, all-important means of livelihood.

During the Civil War, Confederate forces landed at the inlet and drove a Federal company camped here south to the point of the cape. Local residents fled with them, suffering extreme hardships on the long march, and their homes were ravished and burned. Federal regiments stationed at Hatteras then promptly chased the Confederate troops off the island. History books refer to this affair as the Chicamacomico Races!

Soon after the war, a Lifesaving Station and a post office were built in the northern village now known as Rodanthe. The adjoining town, previously called South Rodanthe, was officially named Waves in 1939. Property there has been purchased for a Chicamacomico Banks Fire Department station. The Ladies Auxiliary is a division of this non-profit State corporation.

Dues for non-resident Associate Members of the Chica-- macomico Banks Fire Department are $2.50 a year from date of registration. Honorary membership for life is automatically and most gratefully accorded those who made a donation of an additional $7.50 or more, which is tax-deductable.

Casseroles, One Dish Meals

CRAB EN CASSEROLE

2 c. flaked crabmeat
3 1/2 c. milk
1 tsp. salt
1 tsp. paprika

3/4 c. cracker crumbs
4 eggs
1 Tbsp. grated onion

Sauce:

4 Tbsp. margarine
2 1/2 Tbsp. flour
1 3/4 c. milk
1 tsp. salt

1/4 c. sherry
1/2 tsp. Worcestershire sauce
1 small can mushroom bits
  and liquid

Beat eggs until frothy, add milk and seasonings and beat until well blended. Add onion, cracker crumbs and crabmeat. Stir. Pour into a greased casserole, dot with butter on top and place in a pan containing water and bake in a slow oven, 325 degrees for about 40 minutes or until custard is firm. Serve with following sauce.

Sauce: Melt the margarine, add flour and blend evenly. Add milk gradually and stir over medium heat until sauce is on the verge of boiling. Add seasonings and mushrooms. Place in top of double boiler and keep warm. Just before serving add the sherry and stir. A very good company dish.

Mrs. S. BowenSmith

RETE'S CASSEROLE

1 lb. ground beef
1 lb. sweet Italian sausage
1 medium can mushroom
  pieces
1 small can pimento
1 (#2) can whole kernel corn
1 Tbsp. chopped onion

1 (#2) can tomatoes
1 small can tomato paste
1 medium jar pimento olives
1/2 bottle catsup
1 tsp. chili powder
1 1/2 pkg. wide noodles
sliced American cheese

Cook noodles until tender and reserve. Fry beef, sausage and onion in a small amount of fat, stirring constantly until meat is nicely browned. Add the rest of the ingredients, including the noodles and stir until well mixed. Pour into a large casserole and top with slices of the American cheese. Bake in 350 degree to 375 degree oven for 30 minutes or until cheese has melted and dish is bubbly and has cooked down somewhat. Serve hot with French bread and a green salad This is an excellent casserole for a group of people.

Rete Osborn

SHRIMP CASSEROLE

2 onions, minced	2 Tbsp. fat or oil
1 green pepper, minced	1/2 tsp. salt
1 can tomatoes	1/2 tsp. celery salt
1 lb. cooked shrimp	1/2 tsp. pepper
1 c. cooked macaroni	1/2 tsp. chili powder

Cook peeled and deveined shrimp for 6 minutes or until tender. Cook macaroni until soft. Saute onion and pepper in fat or frying oil until soft. Add seasonings, then tomatoes and blend. Add cooked shrimp and let simmer for 5 minutes. Place a layer of macaroni in a casserole, then a layer of the shrimp mixture and continue to do so until all is used. Sprinkle with bread crumbs, dot with butter and bake in a moderate oven at 350 degrees for 30 minutes or until casserole is nicely browned.

Mrs. S. BowenSmith

HAM AND NOODLE CASSEROLE

1 lb. ground ham	1 can mushroom soup
1 pkg. wide noodles	grated cheese
	fine bread crumbs

Boil noodles until tender. Dilute mushroom soup with equal amount of milk or half milk and half light cream. Place a layer of noodles in a large greased casserole, top with a layer of ham and continue to do so until all is used. Cover with soup and milk mixture, stir gently with a fork until all is covered with the liquid. Sprinkle with grated Parmesan or American cheese, top with fine bread crumbs and dot with butter. Bake in a moderate oven at 350 degrees for 30 minutes or until casserole is browned and bubbly. Serves 6. This is a good way to use leftover ham.

Mrs. R. L. Hahn

STUFFED CABBAGE MARIE

1 (#2 1/2) can sauerkraut	1 egg
1 c. Minute rice	1 tsp. salt
1/2 lb. sausage meat	1 tsp. pepper
1 head cabbage, 2 to 3 lb.	1 Tbsp. minced parsley
pinch thyme	1 tsp. caraway seed
1 bay leaf	1 apple, cored but not peeled
1 small onion	

Sauce:

2 Tbsp. butter	1 egg yolk
1 1/2 Tbsp. flour	1 c. milk or half milk and half cream

Peel outer leaves from cabbage and slice off some of the bottom of the head so cabbage will stand evenly. Slice from the top, 2 inches, with knife score out the inner part of the cabbage until only a shell of outer leaves remains. Wash and reserve. Chop very finely the inside part which has been removed along with the onion. Mix in the raw rice, sausage meat, seasonings and egg, but not the caraway seed or apple. Fill the cabbage head with this mixture. Place in a large kettle the sauerkraut, caraway seed and apple, stir and place on top of this the filled cabbage. If necessary, add enough water to the kettle so that the bottom of the cabbage is covered. Simmer for 2 1/2 to 3 hours or until cabbage is soft.

Serve with Sauce: Melt butter, add flour and blend. Add milk gradually and cook until thick. Just before serving, add the egg yolk and stir until well mixed. Pour sauce over each serving of the filled cabbage. This is a dish for a cold winter's day.

Marie Stretz

CHINESE EGGS

1/2 c. cooked rice
4 hard-cooked eggs
1 c. grated cheese
2 Tbsp. minced green
  pepper

2 Tbsp. canned tomatoes
3/4 c. milk
1 Tbsp. minced onion
1 tsp. salt
1/4 tsp. pepper

Season cooked rice with salt and pepper and spread on bottom of casserole. Halve the hard-boiled eggs lengthwise, remove the yolks and mash with 1/4 cup of the grated cheese, green pepper, onion, tomato pulp and seasoning to taste. Stuff the egg whites with this mixture and arrange on top of the rice. Pour around the eggs a white sauce made with the milk and remaining cheese, cooked in a double boiler until the cheese has melted. Place the casserole in a moderate oven, 350 degrees, for 20 minutes or until it is well heated and the eggs begin to brown. Serves 6.

Mrs. C. C. Alfar

DEVILED EGGS IN CASSEROLE

6 hard-boiled eggs
2 1/4 c. white sauce
1 tsp. prepared mustard
1/4 tsp. Worcestershire
  sauce
dash Tabasco sauce

1/4 tsp. salt
1/4 tsp. pepper
1/4 tsp. cayenne pepper
Parmesan cheese
bread crumbs

Halve the eggs lengthwise and reserve the whites. Mash the yolks with all ingredients and 1/4 cup of the white sauce. Stuff the mixture into the whites and press halves together. Put into a greased casserole, pour over the rest of the white sauce, sprinkle with cheese and crumbs and bake in a hot oven (400 degrees) for 15 minutes or until top is nicely browned. This is a good luncheon dish when served with a green salad.

Bertha P. Anderson

CHICKEN BAKED IN CREAM

1 frying chicken	1/2 lb. mushrooms
1 Tbsp. minced onion	milk
1/2 c. butter	2 c. light cream
flour	salt and pepper to taste

Cut chickens into serving pieces, dip into the milk and then in the seasoned flour and brown in a skillet on all sides. When nicely browned, remove to a casserole and keep in reserve. Saute mushrooms and minced onion in butter in the skillet until soft and scraping the brown particles in the pan. Pour over the chicken in the casserole, add the warmed cream, cover and bake in a moderate oven at 350 degrees for one hour or until chicken is tender. Serve with hot steamed rice.

Mrs. C. C. Alfar

CHICKEN-CORN CASSEROLE

1/4 c. butter	1 Tbsp. grated onion
1/2 c. flour	2 c. diced chicken
2 1/2 c. chicken broth	1/2 c. grated American cheese
1 tsp. salt	1 Tbsp. chopped pimento
1/8 tsp. pepper	buttered bread crumbs

Melt butter and blend in flour, stir in chicken broth and cook over medium heat until thick, stirring constantly. Add salt, pepper and grated onion, blending all ingredients thoroughly. Add the diced chicken, corn, cheese and pimento, stir. Pour into a 2-quart casserole and top with the buttered crumbs. Bake in a moderate oven at 350 degrees until bubbly and top is nicely browned. Serve at once.

Mrs. Camille Midgett

VEGETABLE CASSEROLE

1/2 c. cooked string beans	1 c. white sauce
1/2 c. cooked carrots	2 Tbsp. grated cheese
1/2 c. diced celery	1 tsp. salt
1/2 c. canned corn	1 tsp. pepper
1/2 c. canned peas	1 small onion, grated
1/2 c. bread crumbs	

Butter a large casserole. Place vegetables in layers with a bit of the white sauce between the layers. Add seasoning, top with crumbs and cheese and bake in a moderate oven, 350 degrees, for 30 minutes. Leftover vegetables may be used in this way, and mushrooms may be added also, using some of the mushroom liquid in making the white sauce. This is a nice dish for spring-time vegetables.

Mrs. C. C. Alfar

STEAK AND ONION PIE

1/3 c. shortening	3 tsp. salt
1 1/2 c. sliced onions	1/4 tsp. pepper
1 1/2 lb. round steak, cut into 1/2 inch pieces	3 1/4 c. boiling water
	1 Tbsp. Worcestershire sauce
1/3 c. flour	1 c. raw potatoes, diced

Melt shortening in skillet, add onions and saute gently until golden. Remove onions and reserve. Roll pieces of meat in flour, salt and pepper and sear in skillet until nicely browned. Add boiling water and Worcestershire sauce and sprinkle any remaining flour mixture over meat. Stir, cover and simmer until meat is tender, about 1 hour. Add diced potatoes, cook for 10 minutes longer. Roll "Water-Whip" pastry dough into shape to line baking dish, pour hot meat mixture in and place cooked onions on top. Use remaining pastry to cover pie, careful to seal edges tightly. Cut a vent in the top and bake in a hot oven at 450 degrees for 25 to 30 minutes or until pastry is a golden brown. Makes 6 servings.

Mrs. L. B. Anderson

WELCOME TO

Fair Haven Methodist Church

BETWEEN RODANTHE & WAVES

SUNDAY SCHOOL: 10:00 A.M.

WORSHIP SERVICE: 11:00 A.M.

THIRD SUNDAY EACH MONTH:

WORSHIP SERVICE: 9:30 A.M.

SUNDAY SCHOOL: 11:00 A.M.

Soups, Salads

CHICAMACOMICO STYLE OYSTER STEW

1/4 lb. salt pork, cooked
   crisp
1 qt. water

1 qt. oysters and juice
salt and pepper to taste

Fry diced salt pork until crisp, add rest of ingredients, bring to boiling point and cook for 15 minutes, reducing heat to moderate. Butter or margarine may be substituted for salt pork, if desired. Serve hot in bowls with oyster crackers.

Mrs. Asa Gray, Jr.

MINCED CLAM SOUP

2 cans minced clams
1 can celery soup
2 cans water
salt and pepper to taste

1 c. diced potatoes
1 small onion, minced
1 Tbsp. butter or 1 Tbsp.
   bacon drippings

Place all ingredients into a large kettle, season to taste and bring to a boil. Cook until the potatoes are soft. Makes 3 generous servings.

Mrs. Sarah Midgett

YANKEE CLAM CHOWDER

18 large clams
6 medium onions
6 large potatoes
salt and pepper to taste

1 pt. additional clam juice
2 Tbsp. salt pork scraps
equal amounts of milk and
   light cream

Chop, but do not grind the clams. Saute the diced onions in salt pork scraps until golden brown. Boil diced potatoes until semi-soft, reserving 1 cup of the potato water. Combine these ingredients and simmer slowly but do not boil. Add salt and pepper, stir in extra clam juice. Remove from fire, cool and store in refrigerator overnight. When ready to serve, add equal amounts of milk and cream. Bring to a boil and serve. Serve with saltines. Up in New England from whence came my father's people, this chowder was always served for Sunday evening suppers, so that everyone would arrive at church meeting on time.

Mrs. L. Anderson

CLAM CHOWDER

25 clams	1 tsp. salt
3 slices salt pork	1/2 tsp. pepper
4 c. diced potatoes	1 qt. water
2 c. diced onion	flour

Fry pork in pan, when nicely brown, add chopped clams. Remove to larger pot, add potatoes, onions, salt and pepper and water. Cook until clams are tender. Mix a little flour with some cold water, stir into the chowder and cook just long enough until it has thickened. Serve with crackers.

Ruby Toler

CHICAMACOMICO STYLE CLAM CHOWDER

1/4 lb. salt pork	8 medium potatoes, diced
3 qt. hot water	1 qt. clams, ground
juice from clams	salt and pepper to taste
4 medium onions, diced	

Run clams through meat grinder until finely ground. Fry salt pork until lightly browned. Add clam juice and water, onions, potatoes and clams. Season with salt and pepper. Cook over medium heat for about 3 hours. If necessary, a small amount of water may be added.

Mrs. Asa Gray, Jr.

CHICAMACOMICO STYLE CLAM CHOWDER

1 qt. clams	8 slices salt pork
2 potatoes	2 Tbsp. corn meal
2 onions	

Drain the clams from juice and chop very fine. Peel, dice potatoes and onions. Place in large soup kettle, add salt pork drippings and cook 1 hour. Mix corn meal with enough water so it can be put into the soup. Stir in and cook for 5 minutes.

Mrs. Zenovah Hooper

MELLIE'S SPECIAL CLAM CHOWDER

1 c. minced clams	2 c. fresh milk
1 c. potatoes, diced	1 tsp. garlic salt
1/2 c. onions, diced	1 tsp. onion salt
	dash parsley

Cook over slow heat 1 hour.

Mellie Edwards

SPLIT PEA SOUP

1 lb. dried green split peas	3 qt. cold water
1 lb. smoked pork or ham	1 grated onion
bone with some meat on it	1 grated carrot

Pick peas and wash and soak in cold water overnight. Drain peas and put in heavy kettle with the 3 quarts of water, onion and carrot. Cook over medium heat for 1 hour, skimming occasionally. Lower heat to simmer, cook covered for 2 hours, or until meat is tender and peas are pureed. Season soup with some ground ginger, salt if needed, freshly ground black pepper to taste. Serve in bowl with some of the meat to each portion, adding croutons on top of the soup.

Mary Fellse

OLD-FASHIONED LENTIL SOUP WITH FRANKS

1 pkg. dried lentils	1 stalk celery, diced
1 slice bacon, minced	6 qt. water
1 onion, diced	4 Tbsp. flour
1 carrot, diced	1 pkg. frankfurters, cut into
1 tsp. salt	slices
1/2 tsp. pepper	

Wash and pick over lentils, rinse in water. In a heavy soup kettle, saute the bacon bits with the onion until light brown. Add flour, stir until well mixed and gradually add water, stirring constantly until mixture is smooth and free from lumps. Stir in lentils, carrot and celery, add salt and pepper and cover. Simmer slowly for 3 to 4 hours or until lentils are soft and soup thickens. Ten minutes before serving, add sliced franks, cook for 5 minutes more and serve. Serves 8. This soup is just as good the next day, and it may also be frozen for later use.

Mrs. L. Anderson

CHICAMACOMICO STYLE NAVY BEAN SOUP

1 lb. small navy beans	1/2 lb. salt pork
2 qt. water	salt and pepper to taste

Wash beans and run through water until they are white. Put in soup kettle with the water, add salt pork and boil slowly in a covered pot for about 3 hours. Season with salt and pepper. Makes about 6 servings. Very good served with chopped onions and hot biscuits.

Mrs. Asa Gray, Jr.

CRABMEAT RAVIGOTE

1 lb. lump crabmeat
1 tsp. salt
1/8 tsp. cayenne
1 tsp. prepared mustard

1 Tbsp. olive oil
3 Tbsp. lemon juice
2 Tbsp. minced parsley
Ravigote Mayonnaise

Ravigote Mayonnaise:

1 c. mayonnaise
1 Tbsp. tarragon vinegar
dash cayenne

1 tsp. minced parsley
1 tsp. minced onion

Carefully combine all ingredients except for the mayonnaise. Pile in baking shells. Chill thoroughly and just before serving, coat with Ravigote Mayonnaise.

Ravigote Mayonnaise: Mix all ingredients together until they are well blended and smooth. Chill until ready to use on crabmeat.

Berta Anderson

CRABMEAT SALAD DELUXE

1 c. salad dressing
1 Tbsp. heavy cream
1/2 tsp. curry powder
1 Tbsp. minced parsley
1/4 c. chili sauce

2 Tbsp. sherry
2 Tbsp. lemon juice
1/4 tsp. pepper
3 lb. lump crabmeat
lettuce hearts

Mix all ingredients except for crabmeat and lettuce. Fold crabmeat carefully into the mixture, being careful not to break the lumps. Put in bowl and chill thoroughly for 2 hours. Serve in lettuce hearts and garnish with lemon wedges, stuffed olives and minced parsley on top. Serves 10.

Berta Anderson

SHRIMP SALAD

1 lb. shrimp, cooked
  (boiled)
2 c. cooked macaroni
1 small green pepper

2 medium onions, chopped
1/4 c. chopped celery
1 dash garlic salt
salt and pepper to taste

Toss with mayonnaise to desired consistency.

Bette Gray

COTTAGE CHEESE RINGS

2 c. cottage cheese
3/4 tsp. salt
1 tsp. sugar
1 Tbsp. lemon juice
1/2 c. cream

1 Tbsp. gelatin
1/4 c. cold water
lettuce
fruit or vegetable salad

Combine cottage cheese, salt, sugar, lemon juice and cream. Sprinkle gelatin over the water and let stand for a few minutes until softened. Place over boiling water until dissolved. When gelatin is cool, pour into the cheese mixture. Pour into a salad ring which has been rinsed in cold water, set in refrigerator until firm. Unmold on lettuce leaves and fill center with either a fruit salad or a vegetable salad. Top with mayonnaise. Serves 6.

Mary Preston

FRUIT SALAD

9 oranges, peeled and
  sectioned
2 grapefruit, peeled and
  sectioned
2 apples, sliced but not peeled

lettuce
1/2 c. cottage cheese
1/2 lb. sweet cherries,
  pitted and halved

Sour Cream Dressing:

1 c. mayonnaise
1 c. sour cream

dash Tabasco sauce
1 tsp. parsley flakes

Arrange alternate sections of orange, grapefruit and apple slices in a fan shape on lettuce leaves. Place a spoonful of cottage cheese on one half a cherry and top with the other half. Place filled cherries in center of salad. Serve with a sour cream dressing. Serves 4.

Dressing: Mix all ingredients together and chill. Serve in a separate dish from salad.

Mary Preston

FIVE CUP SALAD

1 c. pineapple pieces
1 c. orange pieces
1 c. sour cream

1 c. marshmallows, cut into
  small pieces
1 c. grated coconut

Blend all ingredients into the sour cream with a fork, being careful not to break up the fruit. Chill for 2 or more hours before serving on a bed of crisp lettuce. A cherry may be added to the salad before serving, along with a small amount of mayonnaise. Good on a hot day with cheese straws.

Mrs. Virginia O'Neal

PEAR AND ROQUEFORT SALAD

3 oz. cream cheese
3 large pears
salt and pepper to taste

1/4 lb. Roquefort cheese
1/4 c. butter

Soften cream cheese with enough cream to make a dressing of the consistency of heavy cream and season with salt and pepper to taste. Peel, halve and core pears, remove stems and rub fruit with a cut lemon to prevent browning. Arrange pears on lettuce, cut side up. Beat Roquefort cheese and butter until mixture is smooth and press into the cavities of each pear. Coat each pear with cream cheese dressing, sprinkle tops with paprika and chill thoroughly.

Berta Anderson

LOBSTER SALAD

1/2 c. mayonnaise
1/2 c. diced celery
1/8 tsp. pepper
1/4 tsp. salt

2 lb. cooked lobster, cut in
  small pieces
1/2 tsp. onion flakes

Place all ingredients into salad bowl, toss with a fork lightly until well blended and serve very cold. Also delicious served on crackers or Melba toast.

Alethia M. Meekins

CHERRY COLA MOLD

1 pkg. (8 oz.) cream cheese
1/2 c. mayonnaise
1 (3 oz.) pkg. cherry jello
1 (3 oz.) pkg. strawberry
  jello
1 c. chopped nuts

1 c. boiling water
1 can pitted dark sweet
  cherries
1 can pineapple tidbits
1 (7 oz.) cola beverage

Soften cream cheese to room temperature, add mayonnaise and blend until smooth. Dissolve the jello in the boiling water, stir into the cream cheese mixture. Drain cherries and pineapple, reserving 1 1/2 cups of the syrups. Add fruit syrups and cola beverage to the gelatin mixture. Place in refrigerator and when almost set, fold in the fruits and nuts. Return to refrigerator and chill until firm and set. Use a 1 1/2 quart mold and it will make about 6 cups or 12 servings.

Mrs. Elma June Torge

TUNA SPRING SALAD

2 Tbsp. chopped olives	1/2 c. shredded carrot
2 c. cottage cheese	1/2 c. chopped celery
1/3 c. sour cream	1 (7 oz.) can tuna
2 tsp. chopped onion	1 Tbsp. vinegar
1/4 tsp. Worcestershire	salt and pepper to taste
sauce	2 Tbsp. minced parsley
lettuce	

Mix olives, carrots, celery, parsley, onion and vinegar. Mix cottage cheese and Worcestershire sauce. Drain tuna fish from oil and break into large flakes with fork. Add vegetables and cheese mixture. Toss lightly. Season with salt and pepper and serve on lettuce leaves. Serves 4.

Mary Preston

GERMAN POTATO SALAD

medium size potatoes	2 Tbsp. vinegar
4 slices bacon	salt and pepper to taste
1 onion, sliced	

Peel and cook and drain potatoes. Cut into very thin slices. Put into a shallow baking dish and season with salt and pepper. Dice the bacon slices and fry in a skillet along with the chopped onion. When onion is getting soft, add the vinegar and allow to come to boiling point. Pour over the potatoes, toss lightly with a fork so dressing coats the potatoes. Cover and let stand in a slow oven, 300 degrees, until warmed through. Serve while warm. Decorate with slices of hard-boiled eggs.

Mrs. Bounce Anderson

Rolls – Breads

MR. LOUIS' CORN BREAD

4 stale biscuits
2 c. white corn meal
1 tsp. baking powder
2 Tbsp. molasses

2 eggs, beaten
1/2 c. sweet milk
1 tsp. baking soda
1/2 tsp. salt

Break biscuits in small pieces and soak until soft in a small amount of hot water. Beat eggs slightly, add milk and molasses. To the corn meal, add the baking powder and baking soda, stir in soaked biscuits and mix well. Gradually add the wet ingredients and stir until well blended. Pour into a greased pan and bake until firm to touch in a moderate oven (350 degrees).

A. Louis Midgett

HUSH PUPPIES

3/4 c. corn meal
1 tsp. salt
1 tsp. sugar
1/4 c. flour
hot fat

1 tsp. baking powder
1 egg, beaten
1 small onion, grated
milk

Mix sufficient milk with the corn meal until it is of medium thickness. Stir in rest of ingredients and mix until well blended. Have ready a pot of hot fat. Drop corn meal mixture in fat by spoonfuls, turning when one side is brown and cook until they are browned on all sides. Serve at once.

Ruby Toler

BUTTERMILK CORN STICKS

1 c. buttermilk or 1 c.
  sour milk
1/2 tsp. baking soda
1 egg, beaten

1 Tbsp. sugar
1/2 tsp. salt
3/4 c. yellow corn meal

Combine buttermilk and soda. Stir in egg, sugar and salt. Add corn meal, a little at a time, mixing well after each addition. Fill greased corn stick pans 3/4 full with batter. Bake at 450 degrees for 12 to 15 minutes or until golden brown. Makes 10 corn sticks. This bread loves butter; lay on plenty of it. It's good with most everything!

Alethia M. Meekins

BIRDIE'S CORN CAKES

3/4 c. water-ground white
  corn meal
1/4 c. flour
1/2 tsp. salt
1/8 tsp. baking soda

1/4 c. bacon drippings
1/2 c. sour milk or 1/4 c.
  buttermilk and 1/4 c.
  water

Sift together the corn meal, salt and baking soda. Mix in the sour milk (or buttermilk and water) and stir in bacon drippings. The batter should be thin enough so edges of the cakes will be lacy. Bake cakes on a skillet in enough heated oil until they are brown and crisp on all sides.

Birdie C. Plum

OLD FASHIONED PONE BREAD

3 c. plain corn meal
2/3 c. flour
2 Tbsp. molasses
2 qt. very hot water (just below boiling)

1/2 c. sugar
1/2 tsp. baking soda
1/2 tsp. salt

Mix corn meal and flour together. Pour over this mixture the hot water and stir until well mixed. Cover with a cloth and let stand in a warm spot for 12 hours. Next day, add sugar, salt, molasses and baking soda. Mix until well blended and pour into a greased pan. Bake 2 hours in a 350 degree oven. Just as delicious cold as it is hot.

Mrs. Cedric Midgett

SUPPAWN
(Spoon Bread)

1 c. corn meal
1 1/2 tsp. salt
1 1/2 tsp. sugar
1 1/3 c. boiling water

1/4 c. butter
3 eggs, beaten
1 Tbsp. baking powder
1 1/3 c. milk

Combine corn meal, salt and sugar, add boiling water gradually, stirring all the while. Stir in the butter, mix until butter is melted and set aside until cool. Beat eggs until light and foamy and stir into the corn meal mixture with the baking powder. Stir in the milk, blend and pour the batter into a greased baking dish. Set baking dish in a larger pan containing water and bake in a moderately slow oven, 325 degrees, for 15 to 20 minutes, or until set. Serve hot with plenty of butter. The name "Suppawn" is an Indian one meaning "corn porridge".

Bertha P. Anderson

HUSH PUPPIES

3/4 c. meal
1/4 c. flour
1 tsp. baking powder

1 Tbsp. sugar
1/4 tsp. salt
1 small onion

Mix with milk to form ball. Drop into deep fat.
I used this recipe for seven years in a restaurant.

Mellie Edwards

OLD FASHIONED CORN BREAD

2 c. white water-ground
  corn meal
1 tsp. salt

1 1/2 c. water
shortening (lard, Crisco, etc.)

Mix corn meal and salt, stir in water and beat until well blended. Take an iron skillet, in it place shortening and melt over hot heat. When shortening is hot enough pour batter by spoonfuls into the fat, flatten with the back of a spoon, turn down heat, fry until crisp and brown. Serve hot with butter and enjoy it!

Mrs. Colenda Midgett

BAKED CORN BREAD

1 1/2 c. white corn meal
1 slice bread
2 c. milk
3 tsp. baking powder

3 heaping tsp. sugar
1 tsp. salt
2 eggs
1/2 stick margarine

Add meal, baking powder, sugar to bread, which has been soaked in one cup of milk. Stir with spoon, then add other cup of milk and mix well. Add eggs, one by one, and beat well after each addition. Put margarine in iron skillet, place skillet into hot oven, 425 degrees, until margarine is melted. Remove from oven, pour over the corn meal mixture the melted margarine, then pour the meal mixture into the skillet, spooning over the top of meal mixture the margarine, which rises to the top. Bake in hot oven, 425 degrees, for 30 to 40 minutes, watching carefully until the bread is set. Serve hot with plenty of butter.

Mary Hooper

SESAME BISCUITS

1/2 c. sesame seed
2 c. flour
1 tsp. baking powder

1/2 tsp. salt
1/2 c. butter
1/4 c. milk

Put sesame seed on a sheet and put in a 350 degree oven, toast until golden brown. Sift together flour, baking powder and

92

salt. Cream butter until soft, add dry ingredients and sesame seed and mix well. With a fork gradually add and stir in milk and mix until dough can be handled. Roll out on lightly floured board very thin, cut into small squares. Bake in moderate oven at 350 degrees for 8 to 10 minutes or until brown. Serve hot with salads.

Bertha P. Anderson

CINNAMON AND NUT BUNS

2 c. flour
3 tsp. baking powder
1/2 tsp. salt
5 Tbsp. shortening
1/2 c. chopped nuts

2/3 c. milk
softened butter
brown sugar
cinnamon

Mix and sift flour, baking powder and salt. Cut in shortening with pastry blender. Stir in milk and work into a light dough. Roll out on floured board into a sheet, 6 x 8 inches. Spread with the softened butter, sprinkle with cinnamon and nuts. Roll dough as for jelly roll and slice roll crosswise. Put rolls close together in a well greased pan or in greased muffin pans. Bake in a hot oven, 400 degrees, for about 12 minutes or until brown. Serve hot with plenty of butter.

Mrs. Bounce Anderson

HOME-BAKED BISCUITS

1 qt. bread flour
2 tsp. baking powder
1/2 tsp. salt

1 heaping Tbsp. shortening
1/2 c. milk
1/2 c. water

Sift flour, baking powder and salt. Work in shortening, gradually add water and milk. Mix dough until it is firm enough to handle. Roll out dough on lightly floured board, cut with a cookie cutter into rounds and put on buttered sheet. Bake at 450 degrees until brown, about 10 to 12 minutes. Serve hot with plenty of butter and jam.

Mrs. Esta Gray

CHEESE PUFFS

3/4 c. grated Swiss cheese
2 c. white sauce
3 egg whites

1 tsp. cayenne pepper
hot fat

Add cheese to hot thick white sauce and season with cayenne pepper, stir until cheese is melted and let cool. Beat egg whites until stiff and fold gently into cheese sauce mixture, but do not overmix. Have ready deep hot fat. Drop by spoonfuls into the fat and cook until well browned on all sides and they have puffed up. Serve hot with soups and salads or as an appetizer.

Bertha P. Anderson

PARMESAN CHEESE TWISTS

1 c. grated Parmesan cheese	1/4 c. butter
1 c. sifted flour	1/2 tsp. salt
7 Tbsp. sour cream	1 tsp. paprika

Place all ingredients together in a small bowl and work together until dough is smooth. Chill in refrigerator for 30 minutes. On a lightly floured board roll out the dough about 1/4 inch thick, cut into strips 1/2 inch wide and about 9 inches long. Twist the strips into spirals. Put twists on unfloured ungreased baking sheet and bake in moderate oven at 350 degrees for 15 minutes or until a golden brown. Serve hot with salads. Dough may be frozen and kept for 2 to 3 months. When ready to use, remove from freezer 2 hours ahead and proceed as above.

Bertha P. Anderson

BANANA BREAD

2 eggs, well beaten	2 c. flour
1/2 tsp. baking soda	1/2 c. shortening
3 mashed bananas	1 c. sugar

Cream shortening until soft, add sugar and beat well. Add beaten eggs and stir. Sift flour with baking soda and add to egg-shortening mixture. Fold in mashed bananas and mix until well blended. Pour into a greased loaf pan and bake at 350 degrees for 1 hour or until a nice golden brown. May be served warm with butter, or served as a dessert with a tart lemon sauce. Good either way.

Mrs. Virginia O'Neal

HOT RAISED ROLLS

6 1/2 to 7 c. flour	2 yeast cakes
2 c. milk	1/4 c. butter
3 Tbsp. sugar	1/4 c. warm water

Dissolve yeast cakes in warm water. Scald milk, add butter and let melt. Cool. Sift flour and sugar together. When milk-butter is cool enough, add the dissolved yeast to it, and gradually pour into the flour and sugar mixture. Work until dough is smooth, adding more flour if needed. Turn out on floured board, knead slightly, roll out to about 1/2 inch thickness and cut into rounds. Place on greased sheet, let rise in warm place until double in bulk and bake in moderately hot oven, 350 degrees, until a nice golden brown. Serve hot with plenty of butter.

Mrs. Sudie Payne

BIRDIE'S BREAD

1 1/2 c. scalded milk	1 1/2 c. water
1/4 c. shortening	3 pkg. dry yeast
1/4 c. sugar	3 eggs, beaten
6 Tbsp. salt	9 c. enriched flour

Combine first 4 ingredients and stir until fat is melted. Cool to lukewarm by adding the water. When tepid, add the dry yeast which has been softened in a spoonful of the milk mixture and blend well. Blend in the eggs which have been beaten slightly; add gradually the flour, mixing until dough is well blended. This dough is somewhat softer than a kneaded dough and may or may not be chilled. To chill, cover and store in refrigerator until needed. If not chilled, rising time is cut in half. Shape dough into 3 loaves on floured board and place into greased bread pans and cover and put in warm place to rise until double in bulk. Bake in moderate oven at 350 degrees for 1 hour. Dough may also be used for pan rolls by pinching pieces size of a walnut and let rise until double in bulk. Put a dot of butter on each roll before baking. Dough will keep in refrigerator 10 days to 2 weeks.

Birdie Anderson

* * * * * *

Meats, Poultry

CHICKEN WITH GARLIC SAUCE

3 1/2 lb. frying chicken	1/2 c. finely chopped parsley
1/2 c. butter	5 garlic cloves, mashed

Cut chicken into serving pieces and sprinkle with salt and pepper to taste. In a heavy skillet saute the chicken in 1/4 cup of the butter until pale gold on all sides. In a bowl cream the rest of the butter with the parsley and crushed garlic until well mixed. Put the creamed mixture on top of the chicken and cover the skillet tightly and cook over low heat for 30 minutes or until tender. Put chicken in serving platter and pour over it the sauce. Serves 4.

Mrs. L. Anderson

CHICKEN WITH BISCUITS

3 lb. frying chicken	1 can cream of chicken soup
1/2 tsp. salt	1 can biscuits
1/4 tsp. pepper	

Cut chicken into serving pieces and place in large frying pan. Add salt and pepper. Add the chicken soup and put in the oven at 350 degrees and bake for 1/2 hour, covering the pan tightly. When tender, remove from oven, place biscuits on top of chicken and return to oven and bake until biscuits are nicely browned.

Mrs. Virginia O'Neal

STEWED CHICKEN WITH PASTRY

1 stewing chicken, cut up	1/4 tsp. pepper
1/2 tsp. salt	water

Boil chicken in 3 quarts of water with salt and pepper until tender when tested. In a bowl, mix the flour with 1/2 teaspoon salt and enough water to make a dough stiff enough to roll. Place on a floured board and roll into a thin sheet. Cut into strips, drop into the pot with the chicken and cook for 15 to 20 minutes more. Serve with hot biscuits.

Mrs. Esta Gray

CHICKEN WITH PARMESAN CHEESE

3 1/2 lb. frying chicken	3 egg yolks, beaten
1/4 c. butter	1/2 c. Parmesan cheese
2 Tbsp. flour	1/2 c. dry bread crumbs

2 Tbsp. melted butter   1 Tbsp. Parmesan cheese
3/4 c. light cream

Cut chicken into serving pieces, season with salt and pepper to taste, and saute in 1/4 cup butter, turning frequently, for about 30 to 35 minutes or until tender when tested. In a saucepan blend flour and melted butter and cook until it bubbles. Add the cream, the tablespoon of Parmesan cheese and cook until thick. Add egg yolks, stir and remove from heat. Sprinkle bottom of buttered flameproof dish with the 1/4 cup of Parmesan cheese, lay on chicken pieces and coat with sauce. Bake in moderate oven, 350 degrees, for 10 minutes. Remove from oven, sprinkle with rest of Parmesan cheese and bread crumbs and put under broiler until topping is browned. Serve with a green salad and French dressing.

Mrs. L. Anderson

BARBECUE CHICKEN

2 or 2 1/2 lb. fryer   1 Tbsp. margarine
1 c. hickory smoke barbecue   salt and pepper as desired
  sauce

In large baking dish melt margarine. Cut up fryer as for frying, salt and pepper. Coat each piece well with flour, dip into barbecue sauce diluted with 1/2 cup water, and place in baking dish. Pour remaining sauce over all. Bake in oven at 325 degrees for 1 hour.

Mrs. Cedric M. Midgett

SOUTHERN STYLE FRIED CHICKEN

2 to 2 1/2 lb. chicken   1/2 tsp. salt
1 c. flour   1/2 tsp. pepper
                    hot fat

Disjoint chicken and season with salt and pepper. Put flour into a paper sack, place chicken pieces in the sack and shake well until each piece is thoroughly coated. Have ready cooking oil. Drop pieces in the hot fat, 350 degrees, and cook for about 20 to 25 minutes. Drain on absorbent paper. Makes 6 servings

Mrs. Asa Gray, Jr.

CHICKEN WITH SHERRY

3 1/2 lb. frying chicken	1 c. light cream
1/4 c. butter	1/2 c. sherry
1/2 lb. mushrooms	salt and pepper to taste

Cut chicken into serving pieces, sprinkle with salt and pepper and a bit of paprika, dust with flour and saute in butter, turning pieces occasionally to brown on all sides. Add mushrooms, sliced, and cook for 5 minutes. Transfer to casserole. Into the chicken skillet, pour the cream, scraping and blending the brown particles in the pan, and cook for several minutes. Stir in the sherry and pour the sauce over the chicken. Cover and bake in a moderately slow oven, 325 degrees, for 50 to 60 minutes, or until tender when tested. Serves 4.

Mrs. L. Anderson

CHICKEN PAPRIKA AND DUMPLINGS

3 lb. fryer	2 tsp. paprika
1/2 pt. heavy cream	salt and pepper to taste
2 Tbsp. butter	2 Tbsp. flour

Dumplings:

2 c. milk	3 c. flour
2 eggs	1/2 tsp. salt

Chicken: In a large pot, put in the butter and place over low flame. When butter has turned brown, add disjointed chicken pieces, salt, pepper and paprika. Cover the pot and let simmer for 45 minutes, stirring occasionally and turning chicken so it will brown on all sides. When browned, add about 2 cups water and cook over low heat until tender when tested. Remove chicken from pot, stir in flour to make gravy, add cream and heat to boiling and remove from fire.

Dumplings: Have ready a large pot of boiling salted water. In a bowl, place milk, eggs and salt and beat until well blended. Add the flour and stir until it is a thick paste, adding more flour if necessary. Take up a bit on the tip of a spoon, drop into the boiling water, cook for about 5 minutes. Remove from heat, put in a colander and run cold water over the dumplings until they are firm. Drain. Place chicken on serving platter, set dumplings around and pour over the sauce.

Mrs. Nora E. Herbert

CHICKEN A LA LEMON

3 1/2 lb. frying chicken	1/4 c. butter
3 Tbsp. cooking oil	3 Tbsp. flour
2 large onions, chopped	2 tsp. dry mustard
2 c. water	1/2 tsp. sweet basil
1/2 c. fresh lemon juice	salt and pepper to taste

Disjoint chicken, dust with flour and saute gently in the cooking oil. Drain from oil and put in baking dish. Saute onion in butter until tender but not brown. Stir in mustard, flour, salt, pepper and basil and mix well. Gradually add water and lemon juice, stirring constantly. Cook until sauce thickens slightly and pour over chicken and bake in moderate oven at 350 degrees for 1 hour, or until chicken is tender when tested. Serve hot with steamed buttered rice.

Bertha P. Anderson

TURKEY SQUARES WITH MUSHROOM SAUCE

3 c. coarsley chopped turkey, cooked	1/2 tsp. salt
	1 Tbsp. lemon juice
2 c. soft bread crumbs	2 Tbsp. minced onion
1 c. turkey broth	1 minced pimento
2/3 c. minced celery	2/3 c. cream
3 eggs, slightly beaten	1/2 tsp. pepper

Mushroom Sauce:

1/4 c. melted butter	1 can chopped mushrooms and liquid
1/4 c. flour	1 c. turkey broth

Mix all ingredients together and pour into a greased baking dish and set dish in a pan of water. Bake in a moderate oven at 350 degrees for 50 to 60 minutes. Cut into squares and serve with Mushroom Sauce.

Mushroom Sauce: In a saucepan melt the butter, add the flour and blend. Heat until mixture is bubbly. Gradually stir in the turkey broth and the mushroom liquid and cook until thick. Add the chopped mushrooms and season to taste with salt and pepper. A pinch of poultry seasoning may be added.

Mrs. L. B. Anderson

STEWED WILD GOOSE

wild goose	1/2 tsp. salt
1 chopped onion	1/4 tsp. pepper
1 Tbsp. butter	1 stalk celery, diced

Clean bird, disjoint into serving pieces and dredge with flour. In a heavy kettle, saute bird in butter or salt pork until golden on all sides. Add onion and celery and water to cover, salt and pepper. Simmer for 2 hours or until bird feels tender when pricked with a fork. Make dumplings, thicken gravy with some flour and serve. If the goose tends to be on the old side, soak in salted water for several hours before stewing.

Mrs. Viola Midgett

ROAST WILD GOOSE

wild goose	raw apples, peeled, cored and
salt and pepper to taste	diced
1 garlic clove	small peeled whole onions
brandy	top of 1 celery stalk

Goose should be drawn and aged for 1 to 2 days. Render the goose fat and keep for pie crust and biscuits. Clean, singe and wipe with damp cloth. Rub with salt, pepper, garlic and a little brandy, both inside and outside of the goose. Fill the cavity with the apples, onions and the celery stalk. Cook in moderate oven, 350 degrees, uncovered until a glossy brown, basting with water if the goose does not make enough liquid in the pan. The drippings may be thickened with a bit of flour for a gravy. Takes about 2 hours.

Mrs. L. Anderson

QUAIL IN CREAM

8 quail, split	salt and pepper to taste
1/2 lb. butter	2 c. fine bread crumbs
1 c. heavy cream	currant jelly

Melt butter in a heavy skillet over medium heat. Gently saute the quail, spooning the butter over them and turning the birds until they are brown, about 30 minutes. Put them on a heated platter and reserve. Into the skillet, pour the cream, scraping all the brown particles in the pan up into the cream. Cook slowly for 5 minutes, add the fine bread crumbs and pour over the birds. Serve 2 quail on a toast point with 1 teaspoon of currant jelly.

Mrs. Bounce Anderson

BAKED WILD DUCK

wild duck
peeled, cored and diced apples

peeled, small whole onions
salt and pepper to taste

Pick, clean and wash duck. Soak in a weak soda (baking) solution for 1 hour. Drain and dry thoroughly. Fill the cavity with the onions, apples, rub the outside of the duck with salt, pepper and a little flour and place in baking pan. Cook in moderate oven, 325 degrees, until tender when tested with a fork, about 2 hours. The duck should be well browned. If duck tends to be on the dry side, add a little water and baste several times during the baking. Serve with sweet potatoes and applesauce.

Mrs. L. Anderson

WILD DUCK

1 wild duck, mallard, red-
   head, teal
3 slices salt pork

2 onions
salt and pepper to taste

Clean, singe and wipe with damp cloth, both the outside and inside of your bird. Have ready the iron kettle, lay a slice or two of the salt pork on the bottom of the kettle, put in the bird, and cover the breast with another slice of pork. Add the sliced onions, salt and pepper, a small glass of water, cover and let stew slowly under moderate heat. If necessary, more water may be added. Cook until tender when tested with a fork. Thicken gravy with flour and pour over the duck.

Mrs. Viola Midgett

WILD GOOSE STEW

1 wild goose, disjointed
2 lb. yellow turnips
2 c. corn meal
salt and pepper to taste

2 c. flour
1/2 lb. salt pork
1 medium onion

Put the goose in a large kettle, cover with water and add the onion, salt and pepper. Cover and cook over low heat, but keep pot boiling at a gentle roll, and if needed, add more water. When goose is half done, place in pot the peeled, sliced turnip (in 8 sections) and continue cooking. When goose is tender, add corn meal mixed with boiling water and made into patties for dumplings, dropped into the goose pot. Add flour mixed with warm water, enough to hold together to roll out, cut into strips and drop into goose pot. Cook 15 minutes longer and serve.

Mary Hooper

HAM TUTTI FRUTTI

1 (2 inch thick) ham steak
1 c. pineapple chunks
1 c. raisins or 1 c.
  cooked prunes
1 c. brown sugar
1/2 c. orange slices
heavy duty foil wrap

Combine pineapple chunks with the raisins or the chopped prunes and half the brown sugar. Spread half of this mixture over one ham steak and top with the other ham steak, sandwich fashion. Take a large piece of heavy duty foil, place the steak on it and wrap loosely. Place the package on a shallow pan and bake in a hot oven at 400 degrees for 45 minutes. Remove package from oven, roll back the top of the foil. Spoon out the fat that has collected in the package. Top the steak with the remaining fruit mixture and remaining brown sugar and return to oven for another 20 minutes to glaze. Unwrap from foil and serve hot.

Mrs. Sarah Midgett

CHOP SUEY

1 1/2 lb. steak
5 to 7 carrots
1 stalk celery
1 1/2 Tbsp. cornstarch
2 Tbsp. fat
2 large onions
2 bell peppers
1 can bean sprouts
2 Tbsp. soy sauce

Fry meat in fat and fat cut off from meat, and cook until half done. Peel and slice carrots, onions, celery and peppers. Add to meat. Drain the juice from the bean sprouts into a bowl, stir in the cornstarch into the liquid and mix until smooth. Re serve. Add the bean sprouts to the meat and vegetable mixture and continue to cook until meat and vegetables are tender. Just before serving, add the cornstarch liquid and the soy sauce, cook for 5 minutes or until thickened and serve with steamed rice and fried noodles.

Ruby Toler

STUFFED PEPPERS

2 lb. chopped meat
2 medium onions, chopped
1 small green pepper,
  chopped
1 small can tomato sauce
1 can tomato soup
6 large green peppers
1/2 tsp. pepper
1/2 Tbsp. vinegar
1/2 tsp. hot peppers
1/2 tsp. oregano
1 Tbsp. Worcestershire sauce
1/2 c. water
3/4 c. rice

In a large skillet, combine chopped meat, onions, salt

pepper. Fry gently until nicely browned. When browned, add tomato sauce and tomato soup, spices and water, simmer gently for 20 to 30 minutes or until mixture thickens. Cut tops from peppers, remove seed and place in boiling vinegar and water and cook until tender. Steam rice until soft. Add to tomato and meat mixture and stir. Drain peppers, place in a casserole and stuff with the rice, meat and sauce combination. Top each pepper with a dash of catsup. Place in moderate oven, 350 degrees, and bake until tops of peppers are brown.

Mrs. Linda Hooper

BEEFSTEAK PIES

Pastry:

3 1/4 c. flour
1 3/4 c. butter
4 egg yolks

2 to 3 Tbsp. cold water
1 egg yolk
1 tsp. cold water

Filling:

1 large onion, chopped
2 Tbsp. oil
2 Tbsp. butter
1 1/2 lb. lean round steak, cubed

salt and pepper to taste
dash Tabasco sauce
1/2 tsp. oregano

Pastry: Sift flour into a mound on pastry board, make a well in the center and put in fat and eggs. Add water and mix ingredients together roughly with the fingers of one hand. Gradually pull in more flour until all is mixed. If dough seems too stiff, add a few drops of water. Chill for several hours.

Filling: Saute the onion in oil and butter until it is soft. Stir in seasonings, meat and cover the pan and cook until meat is tender, over low heat, about 2 hours. On a lightly floured board, roll out the chilled pastry to about 1/8 inch thickness and line six 5-inch pie plates with it. Divide the beef filling among them. Roll out remaining pastry and cover pies. Seal and crimp the edges, brush top of pies with egg yolk and water. Bake in a hot oven, 400 degrees, until pastry is brown, then lower heat to 350 degrees and bake for another 25 to 30 minutes longer, or until pastry is golden brown. Serve hot.

Mrs. R. L. Hahn

STUFFED PORK CHOPS

6 pork chops   1/2 stick margarine
8 slices bread   water
salt and pepper to taste

Season chops with salt and pepper and lay in baking pan. In a bowl, pinch small pieces of the bread, add the margarine, melted in a small amount of warm water, salt and pepper and form into patties. Put a patty on top of each chop, pour hot water into the pan so that it is even with the chops and bake in moderate oven, 350 degrees, for 50 to 60 minutes. Gravy may be thickened with a small amount of flour.

Mary Hooper

BAKED PORK CHOPS

1 large white cabbage   butter
salt and pepper to taste   1/2 tsp. dried sage
1 c. heavy cream   1/2 c. white wine
4 pork chops   1/4 c. Parmesan cheese, grated

Wash, core and cut up cabbage. Soak 1 hour in salted cold water. Drain and rinse in cold water, put in saucepan and sprinkle with salt and pepper to taste. Add cream, bring to a boil and simmer for 30 minutes. Trim excess fat from chops and fry in 2 tablespoons butter until golden brown. Cover, reduce heat and cook slowly until tender. Remove chops, add the sage and wine to skillet and scrape up all browned particles in pan. Add to cabbage. Place a layer of cabbage in a casserole, cover with the chops, use rest of cabbage over the chops, pour on the liquid. Sprinkle with the cheese and dot with butter. Bake in a moderate oven at 350 degrees for about 45 minutes. Makes 4 servings. Serve with fried apple rings.

Mrs. L. B. Anderson

MARINATED POT ROAST

4 lb. rump or top round   1 tsp. peppercorns
3 c. wine vinegar   2 Tbsp. sugar
3 c. water   2 whole cloves
1 onion, sliced   2 Tbsp. oil or lard
1 bay leaf   2 Tbsp. flour
5 to 6 gingersnaps   1/2 tsp. salt

Rub meat with salt and pepper and put in large earthenware bowl or crock. Heat but do not boil vinegar, water, onion and spices. Pour hot mixture over the beef, cool, cover and put in refrigerator for 24 to 48 hours. Turn meat once to other side. When meat is ready, place heavy kettle over heat and melt

lard in it. Remove meat from brine, dry and dredge with flour
and sear in the hot fat, browning all sides. Pour in the marinade
in which the meat has been, cover the kettle lightly and simmer
for 2 to 3 hours or until tender and the marinade has cooked down.
Remove meat and keep warm. Taste gravy in kettle. If too sour,
add a little water, if not sour enough, add a little vinegar.
Crumble in the gingersnaps and stir until the gravy has thickened.
Strain into a bowl and serve separately with the beef and potato
dumplings.

Mrs. Bounce Anderson

STUFFED PEPPERS

1 1/2 lb. beef and pork, ground together	12 green peppers
	salt and pepper to taste
2 Tbsp. uncooked rice	1 large can tomato sauce
1 c. corn flakes	1 or 2 eggs

Mix meat, rice, corn flakes, eggs, salt and pepper together for meat balls. Scoop out insides from peppers and fill
with the meat mixture. Place in pan, pour tomato sauce over and
around and simmer for two hours or until tender. Serve with the
sauce in the pan.

Mrs. Bethany Gray

HAM DREAMS

2 c. ground ham	1/2 tsp. tarragon
1/2 green pepper	1/4 tsp. sage
1 onion	1 Tbsp. minced parsley
1 garlic clove	1 Tbsp. lemon juice
2 hard-boiled eggs	mayonnaise
Parmesan cheese	toast slices
salt and pepper to taste	

Grind ham with deseeded green pepper, onion, garlic,
eggs and seasonings. Mix well in a bowl, add the lemon juice
and enough mayonnaise to bind the mixture. When ready to serve,
toast the bread on one side only, spread the untoasted side with
the ham mixture, spread a bit of mayonnaise on top, sprinkle
with Parmesan cheese and place under broiler heat. Broil until
golden brown. Serve at once very hot. Makes a nice luncheon
dish along with a tossed salad.

Isabel Gaylord

* * * * * *

Seafoods

BACON FLOUNDER

2 small flounder fillets	1 Tbsp. butter
6 strips bacon	salt and pepper to taste
1 (3 oz.) can mushrooms, sliced	

Grease a flat pan with the butter and place the fillets in it, smooth side down. Sprinkle with salt and pepper and cover with bacon strips, crosswise. Place under broiler, not too close to flame, and broil for about 15 minutes. Baste with drippings several times while broiling. When fish starts to crisp around the edges, add mushrooms on top and baste again. Broil for another 5 minutes. Fish should flake easily and be crisp around edges. Serve with lemon slices.

Mrs. B. P. Sonn

BAKED SEA SQUAB
(Blowfish)

6 fingers	1/2 tsp. pepper
2 small sliced onions	1 Tbsp. chopped parsley
1/2 tsp. salt	2 Tbsp. sherry
1 tsp. butter	

Put into a piece of baking foil, large enough to seal ends, 3 fingers. Add one onion to each package, 1/2 the parsley, 1/2 the sherry and the butter, salt and pepper. Wrap and seal the package. Lay on a baking sheet, bake in moderate oven, 350 degrees for 15 minutes. Open the foil, put on a plate and pour over the fish the gravy in the package. You may also serve this fish with a rich cream sauce.

Few people know that this fish has a most delicate flavor and is highly prized by gourmets. Fish fingers may also be dipped in egg and crumbs and French fried for five minutes.

Mrs. L. Anderson

BAKED BLUEFISH

4 lb. bluefish	2 Tbsp. salt
5 medium potatoes, sliced	1 tsp. pepper
2 medium onions, sliced	8 slices salt pork
1/3 c. flour	water

Place dressed and scored fish in a greased baking pan. Rub in salt and pepper on top of fish. Place potatoes and onions around fish and in head. Try out salt pork and pour drippings over the fish, putting the slices of pork on the top of the fish.

Place in preheated oven, 400 degrees, and bake for 1 hour. Re-move pan from oven, add flour and water, stir well and cook for 5 minutes. Serve with hot biscuits or corn bread.

Mrs. Zenovah Hooper

BAKED FISH

fish, such as bluefish,
   flounder, gray trout
salt

milk
corn flakes, crushed fine

Cut fish into serving pieces, dip into salted milk, using the proportion of 1 tablespoon of salt to 1 cup of milk. Roll in crushed corn flakes and arrange on an oiled baking sheet or pan. Dot with butter. Bake for 10 to 15 minutes at high heat, 450 de-grees, or until browned and tender.

Mrs. Julian L. Gray

CHICAMACOMICO BOILED OLD DRUM FISH

1/4 side drum fish
12 potatoes
3 Tbsp. salt

1 Tbsp. pepper
1/4 lb. salt pork
2 onions

Scale, clean and cut into pieces the fish. Peel potatoes but leave whole. Put fish and potatoes in large pot, add water to cover and salt and pepper, cover and boil 1 hour. Try out the salt pork.

Chicamacomico style - how to serve: Remove fish to platter, with the potatoes. Dice the onions in a separate bowl, and the salt pork drippings in another bowl. On your plate, then, place a piece of hot steaming drum, and a potato or so, mash them together, add a heaping spoonful of onion and pour over the whole a spoonful of the pork drippings. Add a few hot biscuits or a good slice of corn bread spread with butter, and you have a dish fit for a king.

Mrs. Zenovah Hooper

BAKED BLUEFISH

4 lb. bluefish
4 medium potatoes
2 medium onions
2 slices salt pork

1/3 c. flour
1/2 tsp. salt
1/2 tsp. pepper
water

Scale, dehead and clean fish.

Get your fish and score it,
And roll in flour to make
Tasty gravy for your bake.
And in a big pan put it
With water to the top,
In it salt and pepper drop.
Potatoes and onions peel
And slice pork for your meal.
Put potatoes and onions around the fish,
Pork on top to complete the dish.
Don't forget, please,
Bake in oven, 350 degrees.
When from oven the fish you take,
You'll soon hear,
What a delicious bake.

Mrs. Alethia M. Meekins

BAKED ROCKFISH
(Striped Bass)

5 to 7 lb. rockfish	1 green pepper, chopped
2 large onions, chopped	1/4 c. butter
1 large can tomatoes	bread stuffing

Scale, dehead and clean fish. Saute pepper and onion in butter, add salt and pepper to taste until roux is gently brown. Add tomatoes and cook 5 minutes. Stuff fish with your favorite stuffing, tie cavity if needed to retain stuffing, and lay fish in oiled baking pan. Pour over tomato sauce and bake in moderate oven at 350 degrees for 1 1/2 hours or until fish is tender when tested with fork. Cut into serving pieces and pour some of the gravy over each piece. You may also prepare the fish as above, but omit the tomato mixture. Instead, lay slices of bacon on top of the fish, add a small amount of water to the oiled pan and bake as above. When ready to serve, pour over a cream white sauce with hard-boiled eggs sliced in and a dash of parsley and paprika added to the sauce. Leftover fish, as prepared above, may be mixed with a white sauce enriched with an egg yolk, put into a casserole, the top sprinkled with grated cheese and crumbs and baked until hot and bubbly.

Mrs. L. Anderson

CURRIED FLOUNDER

1 lb. flounder	1/2 tsp. curry powder
2 Tbsp. butter	1 Tbsp. flour
1/2 medium onion, sliced thin	1/4 c. milk

1/2 tsp. salt   1/4 c. white wine
1/4 tsp. pepper

Preheat oven to 350 degrees. Melt half the butter in a fry pan, add salt, pepper, sliced onion, curry powder and wine. Bring to a slow boil, stirring constantly. Place flounder fillets in this mixture, one at a time, and poach lightly on both sides. Remove fillets and place in shallow casserole. Pour sauce into bowl and set aside. Melt remaining butter in the fry pan and stir in flour. Slowly add milk and sauce from first mixing. Bring to boil and stir. Pour sauce over fish and cover. Bake for 15 to 20 minutes or until fish flakes easily. Serve with rice.

Mrs. J. B. Shaw

BAKED FISH WITH SALAD DRESSING

1 fish, flounder, bass,   1/4 c. chopped celery
   bluefish, 2 to 5 lb.   2 chopped tomatoes
1/4 c. butter   1/4 c. minced parsley
1 clove garlic, minced   1 tsp. salt
1/4 c. chopped onion   1/4 tsp. pepper
1/2 c. chopped green pepper   1 tsp. basil

Melt butter in skillet, add garlic, pepper, onion and celery. Cook until tender. Add tomatoes, parsley and seasonings, stir over low heat about one minute. Stuff fish with as much of the mixture as it will hold, pour rest over and around the fish. Bake in a hot oven at 425 degrees, until fish flakes easily when tested with a fork. Allow about 30 minutes for a 2 or 3 pound fish, and about 1 hour for a 5 pound fish.

Mrs. John Manning

CHINESE SWEET AND SOUR FISH

1 (3 to 4 lb.) fish, cut into   2 c. water
   fillets   1 tsp. salt
8 Tbsp. sugar   4 Tbsp. soy sauce
8 Tbsp. vinegar   5 slices ginger
3 Tbsp. sherry   1 scallion
4 Tbsp. cornstarch   flour

Rub flour on fish fillets and deep fry in one inch of fat or oil at high heat for 2 minutes on each side. Turn to medium heat and fry for 4 minutes on each side. The outside should be crisp and the inside soft. Take out of pan and keep warm. Pour off all but one tablespoon of oil from pan. Put in sliced scallion, ginger and other seasonings. Mix cornstarch with water and add this last. Stir over medium flame until mixture becomes clear. Pour over fish and serve.

Mrs. Phillip Ammidown

BAKED BLUEFISH

2 medium size blues	1/2 c. water
2 medium onions, diced	4 slices bacon
4 potatoes, diced	salt and pepper

Wrap in aluminum foil and bake for 3 hours, at 200 degrees. Serves 6.

Bette Gray

FRIED EELS

eels	1 tsp. salt
2 eggs, beaten	1 tsp. pepper
1 oz. melted butter	fine bread crumbs

Clean and cut into pieces the eels. Put in a stew pot and cook until tender. Beat eggs and add salt and pepper to mixture. Roll eel pieces in bread crumbs, dip into egg-salt-pepper mixture and roll again in crumbs. Fry in hot deep fat until golden brown. Serve with lemon wedges.

Mrs. B. P. Sonn

STEWED EELS

eels	1 Tbsp. chopped parsley
1 chopped onion	1 celery stalk, chopped
1/2 tsp. salt	1 Tbsp. flour
1/2 tsp. pepper	1 Tbsp. butter

Clean, skin and remove fat from inside of eels, then cut into 2-inch pieces. Put in pot with enough cold water to cover, add rest of ingredients, cover closely and stew for 1 hour. Melt butter, stir in flour and cook until mixture is blended. Add a little cold water to the roux and add gradually to eel stew and cook until the sauce has thickened. Serve with dumplings.

Mrs. B. P. Sonn

BAKED TUNA

4 lb. tuna	1/4 tsp. thyme
1 c. oil	1 bay leaf
1 c. butter	1/8 tsp. cloves

1 can tomatoes   1 onion, sliced
salt and pepper to taste

Preheat oven to 450 degrees. Put piece of tuna in baking
pan which has been lightly oiled. Pour over the fish the oil, butter
and tomatoes, add the spices. Put the pan in the hot oven and as
soon as the fish has browned, reduce the heat to 350 degrees and
baste with the sauce, cover and bake for 3 hours. If necessary,
a small amount of water may be added through the cooking. Be
sure to baste frequently, so fish remains moist and the good taste
goes all the way through.

Margaret C. Strater

TUNA CASSEROLE

5-inch slice fresh tuna   juice of 1 lemon
equal parts butter and olive   salt and pepper to taste
  oil
small white onions or 4 onions, sliced

Remove skin from piece of tuna, wash and dry. Put in
casserole in which it will fit without cramping, add butter and olive
oil and heat over high flame until fish is nicely browned on both
sides. When fish is about 3/4 finished, add the onions and cook
for 25 minutes over moderate heat, turning fish so it gets brown
all over. Add 1 to 2 cups water, salt and pepper and let continue
to cook for another 15 minutes. Just before it is ready to serve,
pour the lemon juice over the fish. The secret of cooking fresh
tuna is to watch it closely, so that it will not overcook, as this
toughens the fish. So, keep testing with a fork when cooking fresh
tuna.

Mrs. Margaret C. Strater

COLD PACK TUNA

fresh tuna   salt
sterilized jars, rubbers and caps

Soak your tuna in salt water for two or three hours to soak
out blood. Cut into chunks sized to fill quart jars. Pack the
chunks in the jars with the addition of 2 teaspoons salt to each jar.
Half seal the jar. If using a pressure cooker, 1 hour will be
enough to cook. If using boiling water, 3 hours are needed. It
takes approximately 2 pounds of tuna to a quart jar. After this,
you can use this tuna in any way you desire, but it will have much
more taste than commercial canned tuna.

Mrs. Margaret C. Strater

HERRING ROE

8 oz. herring roe
1 egg
salt and pepper to taste

toast
bacon strips

Beat egg. Mash the roe and mix into the egg, stirring until well mixed. Season with salt and pepper. Toast sufficient slices of bread on one side, then spread the roe mixture on the untoasted side. Cover with strips of bacon and broil until bacon is crisp. Delicious for a Sunday morning breakfast.

Mrs. Esta Gray

FRIED OYSTERS

1 pt. oysters
6 Tbsp. flour

2 eggs
salt and pepper to taste

Beat eggs thoroughly, fold in flour, salt and pepper. Mix well. Add oysters and drop by spoonfuls into hot deep fat, 1/4 to 1/2 inch deep. Turn as needed, until both sides are nicely browned. Serve hot, plain as they are cooked, or with catsup.

Mrs. Camille Midgett

SCALLOPED OYSTERS

1 pt. oysters
1 c. milk
1 egg, beaten

1/2 c. melted butter
1/2 tsp. salt and pepper
10 saltine crackers

Beat egg, salt and pepper, add the milk gradually, beating constantly. With a fork, stir in oysters, cracker crumbs and melted butter, then add egg and milk mixture, and blend. Bake in a buttered casserole in hot oven, 400 degrees, for 35 minutes or until browned.

Mrs. C. B. White

OVEN FRIED OYSTERS

1 doz. oysters
1 c. flour
1 tsp. salt
1 tsp. pepper

1 egg, beaten with fork
salad oil
fine bread crumbs

Roll oysters in seasoned flour; dip into egg, roll again in bread crumbs and dip into small amount of salad oil. Bake in a shallow pan in moderate oven, 350 degrees, for about 30 minutes, or until nicely browned. Serve with lemon and tartar sauce.

Mrs. A. H. Dagen

GRILLED OYSTERS

6 oysters per serving   1 tsp. Worcestershire sauce
2 Tbsp. melted butter   salt and pepper to taste

Open oysters but leave in shell; melt butter with Worcestershire sauce, salt and pepper. Pour 1 teaspoon of sauce over each oyster in the shell and set under broiler for 5 minutes, or until the edges of the oyster start to curl. Serve hot with lemon wedges.

Mrs. L. Anderson

STEWED CLAMS

1 qt. clams   6 slices salt pork
2 medium potatoes   2 tsp. salt
2 medium onions   1/4 tsp. pepper

Pastry:

2 c. flour   1 c. water
1 Tbsp. shortening

Remove clams from shell, but do not chop. Peel and slice potatoes and onions. Put clams, potatoes and onions in a large soup kettle, cover with water, add salt and pepper. Try out salt pork and put in drippings. Cook at medium heat 1 hour. Make pastry and mix to a light puffy dough. Roll out in thin strips and cut in 2 inch lengths. Remove from kettle some of the clams, place a layer of pastry, cover with the removed clams and continue to do this until all is used. Cook for 15 minutes more. If stew becomes too dry, add a small amount of water.

Mrs. Zenovah Hooper

QUICK SHRIMP SCAMPI

3 lb. peeled raw and de-   4 minced garlic cloves
  veined shrimp   1/2 c. chopped onion
1/2 c. olive oil or Wesson   salt and pepper to taste
  oil

Saute the shrimp in the oil for 3 minutes, shaking the pan over high heat. Season with salt and pepper and remove to heated dish. Add to the remaining oil in the pan the garlic, some parsley if desired, shake over high heat for a few minutes and pour the sauce over the shrimp. Serve with a green tart salad and green noodles.

Bertha P. Anderson

INDIVIDUAL SHRIMP CASSEROLES

1 lb. shrimp	1/2 tsp. basil
1/4 c. butter	1/2 tsp. tarragon
1/2 tsp. salt	1 tsp. parsley
1 small clove garlic	1/2 c. sherry
Parmesan cheese	bread crumbs

Peel, devein and cook shrimp until pink. Melt butter, add crushed garlic clove and cook for 3 minutes. Remove garlic, add seasonings, shrimp, sherry and stir over low heat until well blended. Place a portion in each individual casserole, sprinkle with Parmesan cheese and bread crumbs and bake in moderate oven at 350 degrees for 10 to 15 minutes, or until heated through. Place under broiler heat for 1 minute or until topping is nicely browned. Serves 4.

Mrs. D. A. Farwell

SCAMPI

1 c. soft butter	2 Tbsp. lemon juice
4 shallots, or 1 onion, chopped	1/2 tsp. salt
4 garlic cloves, crushed	1/2 tsp. pepper
3 Tbsp. steak sauce	1 lb. raw shrimp

Beat first seven ingredients in an electric blender until creamy. Peel and devein shrimp, leaving tails attached. Split shrimp lengthwise, being careful not to cut through the back and spread open. Put the shrimp in a shallow oiled pan, broil for 5 minutes or until cooked through. Arrange in serving dish. Heat seasoned sauce until bubbling but not browned and pour over the shrimp. Serve at once and serve with green noodles.

Mrs. L. Anderson

SHRIMP COOKED IN BEER

3 cans beer	3 lb. raw shrimp
1 tsp. whole cloves	a few celery leaves
1 tsp. chopped parsley	

Wash but do not shell shrimp. Combine all ingredients in large kettle, except for shrimp. When a full rolling boil is reached, add the shrimp. Turn off the heat and cover tightly. When shrimp are cool enough to handle, drain, peel and devein. Serve very cold, plain, or with a catsup-horseradish sauce. May also be used in any dish calling for shrimp. Cooked this way, they have a delicious taste.

Mrs. L. Anderson

CLAM FRITTERS

1 pt. clams (well washed
   and drained)
2 eggs
1/2 c. flour

1/2 tsp. salt
1/2 tsp. pepper
1/2 tsp. baking powder

Chop clams rather fine, stir in eggs, flour, salt, pepper
and baking powder. Drop by tablespoonfuls into hot grease (Crisco
or oil) in skillet and fry until brown on both sides.

Mrs. Cecil L. Midgett

CRABMEAT DEWEY

2 lb. backfin crabmeat
1/4 c. butter
2 c. white sauce
1 c. sliced mushrooms
1 green pepper, cut in strips

1/2 c. sherry
1/2 c. heavy cream
1 slice pimento, cut in
   strips
salt and pepper to taste

Saute crabmeat and pepper in butter for 5 minutes. Combine with white sauce, add salt and pepper and bring to a boil.
Stir in cream and sherry, add pimento and serve. Good with fluffy
rice.

Bertha P. Anderson

CRABMEAT IMPERIAL

1 lb. backfin crabmeat
1/4 lb. butter
1 Tbsp. dry mustard
1 Tbsp. Worcestershire
   sauce
1/2 c. salad dressing
1 Tbsp. prepared mustard

1 tsp. salt
1 tsp. pepper
1/2 green pepper, minced
1/2 red pepper, minced
1 Tbsp. lemon juice
1 egg, beaten

Saute peppers in butter until soft. Add dry ingredients,
lemon juice and egg. Blend, then add crabmeat and stir with fork,
being careful not to break the lumps. Add salad dressing, blend
and fill baking shells with mixture. Sprinkle top with fine bread
crumbs and dot with butter. Bake for 20 minutes in hot oven,
400 degrees, or until well browned. Serve hot with lemon wedges.

Mrs. L. Anderson

CRAB CAKES

1 lb. regular crabmeat
1 egg

1/2 c. cracker meal
dash salt and pepper

Mix together and form cakes; drop in deep fat. Makes 8
cakes.

Mellie Edwards

DEVILED CRABS

1 green pepper, chopped	1/2 tsp. salt
1 small onion, chopped	1/2 c. white sauce
2 Tbsp. butter	1 lb. crabmeat
1 Tbsp. dry mustard	1 Tbsp. fine bread crumbs
1 Tbsp. prepared mustard	

Saute pepper and onion in butter for 10 minutes, stirring vegetables frequently. Remove from fire and stir in remaining ingredients. Heat mixture over low heat, stirring gently. Spoon into 6 baking shells, sprinkle tops with fine bread crumbs and dot with butter. Bake in hot oven, 400 degrees for 10 minutes. Put under broiler flame for a few minutes to brown top. Serve hot with lemon wedges.

Bertha Anderson

DEVILED CRABMEAT

1 1/2 c. milk	1/3 tsp. dry mustard
1 1/2 c. soft bread crumbs	1/8 tsp. cayenne pepper
2 lb. flaked crabmeat	1 1/2 tsp. salt
1/2 c. melted butter	buttered crumbs
5 hard-boiled eggs	

Combine milk and bread crumbs. Gently stir in crabmeat. Slice egg whites and mash egg yolks and add to crab mixture. Add salt, pepper, mustard and melted butter. Pour into a 10 x 6 x 2 inch pan, sprinkle with buttered crumbs and bake at 450 degrees for 20 minutes. Potato chips may be used for topping instead of buttered crumbs.

Mrs. Julian L. Gray

STEAMED CRABS

1 c. vinegar	crabs
1 Tbsp. dry mustard	

Clean crabs. Into a deep pot pour vinegar, add mustard and crabs. Cover lightly and steam until bright red. Chill thoroughly before serving with green mayonnaise.

Mrs. L. Anderson

SAUTEED SOFT CRABS

6 soft crabs, cleaned	bread crumbs
1 egg, beaten	deep fat for frying

Dip crabs in egg, then in fine bread crumbs and drop into

deep hot fat. Fry on both sides until brown and crisp. Serve
with tartar sauce and lemon slices.

Mrs. L. Anderson

CRABMEAT MORNAY

1/4 lb. butter	2 lb. picked backfin crabmeat
1/2 c. flour	1 green pepper, minced
1 pt. milk and cream mixed	1 red pepper, minced
1/2 c. sherry	

Melt butter, add flour and stir roux until blended, slowly
add milk-cream mixture. Stir until thick, stirring constantly.
Add sherry and cook one minute. Set aside. Saute peppers in
small amount of butter until tender. Add crabmeat, cook 1 minute, add to sauce. Cook until mixture is heated throughout.
Serve on toast points or patty shells.

Mrs. L. Anderson

** EXTRA RECIPES **

92

Candies, Cookies

OVERSEAS FUDGE

4 c. sugar   1/4 tsp. salt
1 stick butter   1 tsp. vanilla
1 tall can Pet milk

Cook until it forms a ball, remove from fire and beat in one pint of marshmallow cream, 2 packages chocolate chips and 2 cups nuts.

Mrs. Nora E. Herbert

PEANUT BRITTLE

1 c. corn syrup   1 c. sugar (brown or white)
1 Tbsp. butter   3/4 tsp. salt

Combine above and cook on medium heat until sugar dissolves. Add 1 pound cooked fresh peanuts, stirring constantly until peanuts are light brown. Remove from heat, stirring in quickly 1 teaspoon baking soda, then spread thinly on greased platter. Cool and serve.

Bette Gray

SEAFOAM CANDY

3 c. brown sugar   2 egg whites
1 c. water   1 tsp. vanilla
1 Tbsp. vinegar   1 c. chopped nuts

Mix sugar, water and vinegar together and cook until sugar is dissolved, or until a small ball will form when dropped in cold water. Pour slowly over stiffly beaten egg whites, beating constantly until mixture turns creamy. Add vanilla and nuts, beat again until mixture will hold its shape. Pour into a pan and cut when cool.

Aldean Hayes

PRALINES

1/2 c. dark brown sugar   2/3 c. maple syrup
3/4 c. granulated sugar   chopped pecans

Cook sugars and syrup to soft ball stage, 240 degrees. Allow to cool for three minutes. Stir in chopped pecans, mix and drop by spoonfuls onto a sheet of waxed paper. If mixture starts to harden before all is used, melt it down over boiling water, or add a drop or two of boiling water for smoothness and ease in handling.

Bertha Anderson

BUTTERSCOTCH DROPS

3 pkg. (6 oz. each) butterscotch drops

1 jar dry roasted peanuts
1 can Chow Mein noodles

In a saucepan, melt the butterscotch drops; when all melted, add peanuts and noodles and mix. Drop by spoonfuls onto waxed paper. Allow to set, then store in an airtight container. Makes about 4 dozen pieces.

Mary Fells

FUDGE SUPREME

2 c. sugar
1/2 c. milk
1/2 tsp. salt

2 tsp. cornstarch (heaping)
butter size of a nutmeg
1 tsp. vanilla

Put all ingredients into a saucepan and let melt slowly. Count from time it starts to bubble all over and boil hard for 2 minutes, stirring constantly. Remove from fire and add vanilla and beat until thick, about 7 minutes. If desired, 1/2 cup of chopped nuts may be added. Mark into squares when fudge has set and is cold.

Mrs. Julian Gray

POPCORN BALLS

3 qt. popped corn
2/3 c. molasses
1 1/2 c. sugar
1/2 c. water

1/2 tsp. vinegar
1/2 tsp. salt
2 Tbsp. butter
2 tsp. vanilla

Boil molasses, sugar, water, vinegar, salt together until it becomes brittle when a little is dropped into cold water. Add butter and vanilla. Pour syrup over the popped corn and shape into balls. Dampening the hands with cold water will allow you to form the balls while still hot and will also prevent sticking. Makes 18 balls.

Mrs. Julian Gray

BLACK WALNUT COOKIES

1 c. butter
1 c. confectioners sugar
1 Tbsp. brandy

2 1/2 c. cake flour
1 c. black walnuts, chopped
  finely

Cream butter and sugar until light. Stir in sifted flour, walnuts and brandy and mix until well blended. Drop by spoonfuls on an ungreased baking sheet and bake in a moderately slow oven,

325 degrees, for 15 to 20 minutes, or until golden brown.

Bertha P. Anderson

PEANUT BUTTER COOKIES

1 c. white sugar
1 c. brown sugar
1 c. Karo syrup, white

12 oz. jar peanut butter
5 c. cereal, rice or corn
1 tsp. vanilla

Melt sugars, peanut butter and syrup over low heat, stirring constantly so it will not burn. When all melted, add the cereal and vanilla and mix in well. Spread with back of knife onto a greased cookie sheet and bake in a moderately slow oven, 325 degrees for 15 to 20 minutes. Cookies will be soft and chewy. Cool and then cut into squares.

Mrs. Pat Rollinson

ALMOND CRESCENT COOKIES

1 c. butter or oleo
1/3 c. sugar
1 2/3 c. sifted flour

2/3 c. chopped almonds
1/4 tsp. almond extract
confectioners sugar

Cream butter and sugar together until well blended. Add flour and almonds and extract and mix until dough can be handled. Roll pieces in palm of hand into a long pencil. Chill. Cut into 2 1/2 inch lengths and bend into a crescent shape. Bake in a 350 degree oven for 12 minutes or until the crescents are a golden color. While still warm, roll in confectioners sugar to coat. Keep in a dry container and serve with ice cream. This is a very rich cookie, but most delicious.

Emmy Geotze

ORANGE SAUCEPAN COOKIES

1/2 c. butter or oleo
1/2 c. sugar
1 tsp. grated orange rind
2 Tbsp. orange juice
1 c. sifted flour

1/2 tsp. baking soda
1 egg
1/2 c. chopped nuts
1/2 c. chopped dates

Melt butter in saucepan, remove from heat. Add sugar, rind and orange juice, blend. Stir in sifted flour and soda. Add egg, beat thoroughly. When well mixed, add dates and nuts. Pour batter in a greased 9 x 9 inch cake pan and bake at 350 degrees for 25 minutes. When cool, frost with orange frosting.

Margarette Lotte

ERNA'S COOKIES

1 c. butter or oleo
1/2 c. granulated sugar
1 egg, beaten
1/2 c. milk
rind and juice of 1 lemon

3 c. flour
1/4 tsp. baking powder
1/2 lb. chopped almonds
1/4 tsp. vanilla

Cream butter and sugar together until light in color. Add well beaten egg and milk. Sift together dry ingredients, add slowly to first mixture, beating well after each addition. When all used, add lemon juice, rind and almonds and stir until well mixed. Roll out on floured board, cut with cookie cutter, and bake in a 350 degree oven for 12 minutes or until brown. Sprinkle while still hot with a topping of granulated sugar.

Erna Cooke

STAR COOKIES

6 egg whites
1 lb. confectioners sugar
1/8 tsp. salt

2 Tbsp. cinnamon
1 lb. grated almonds

Beat egg whites until frothy, add sugar, salt and cinnamon, beat in electric mixer for 20 minutes. Save 4 tablespoons of this mixture and put aside. Add almonds to rest of mixture and blend thoroughly. Roll out on sugared board. Cut into star shapes and cover each shape with a bit of the saved icing. Bake in a 350 degree oven for 12 minutes or until a delicate brown. These cookies keep well in a covered container.

Berta Anderson

SOUR CREAM PENUCHE FUDGE

4 1/2 c. brown sugar
2 c. sour cream
1/2 tsp. vanilla

1/4 tsp. salt
1/2 c. seedless raisins
1/2 c. chopped pecans

Place sugar and cream in saucepan, stir until dissolved and bring to boiling point slowly, stirring constantly. Cook to a soft ball stage when a bit is dropped into cold water, remembering that brown sugar takes longer than white. Cool. Add vanilla and salt. Beat until creamy, add raisins and nuts, turn into a greased pan and mark into squares. Keeps well and also ships well.

Mrs. L. Anderson

* * * * * *

Cakes —Frostings

WHIPPED CREAM CAKE

1 c. whipped cream	1 tsp. vanilla
2 eggs, beaten until thick	1 1/2 c. sifted cake flour
and piled softly	1/4 tsp. salt
1 c. sugar	2 tsp. baking powder

Whip chilled cream until it stands in peaks; add beaten eggs and fold together; add vanilla. Sift sugar, flour, salt and baking powder together and fold into egg mixture, a portion at a time. Pour into 2 (8-inch) round layer pans, greased and lined. Bake at 350 degrees about 25 minutes. When cooled, spread Seven Minute Icing.

Seven Minute Icing:

1 unbeaten egg	3 Tbsp. cold water
7/8 c. granulated sugar	1/2 tsp. cream of tartar

Place all ingredients in top of a double boiler. Place over boiling water and beat with beater for seven minutes. Add flavoring, beat and spread on cake.

For Chocolate Icing: Add to above 1 1/2 ounces melted unsweetened chocolate two minutes before taking from heat.

Lourania Midgett

OLD FASHIONED POUND CAKE

1 lb. butter (2 c.)	10 eggs, separated
1 lb. sifted cake flour	1 lb. sugar (2 c.)
(4 c.)	1 tsp. vanilla

Cream butter, work in flour until mixture is mealy. Beat egg yolks, vanilla and half the sugar until thick and lemon-colored. Beat thoroughly into first mixture. Beat egg whites until soft peaks form; gradually beat in rest of sugar; fold into batter; stir until blended. Pour into two 8 1/2 x 4 1/2 x 2 1/2 inch loaf pans, greased and lined. Bake at 325 degrees about 1 1/2 hours.

Mrs. Nora E. Herbert

CHICAMACOMICO CAKE

1 lb. raisins	1/2 c. chopped nuts
1 pkg. dates	2 c. water
1 jar mixed fruit	1 Tbsp. nutmeg
2 c. sugar	1 Tbsp. allspice

3 c. flour   1 Tbsp. cinnamon
1/2 lb. butter

Cook raisins in 1 cup water for 16 minutes, then add 1 cup water, cold. Add sugar with raisins and listed ingredients, except for butter. Melt butter in pan. Mix and pour in pan. Bake 1 hour at 350 degrees.

Ella Midgett

LEMON GELATIN CAKE

1 box lemon cake mix   1/2 c. corn oil
1 box lemon gelatin   4 eggs
2/3 c. milk (evaporated)   1 tsp. vanilla (optional)

Icing:

1 c. sugar   juice of 1 orange
juice of 2 lemons

Cake: Combine all ingredients in order listed. Bake at 325 degrees until tester inserted in center comes out clean.
Icing: Mix and spread while cake is hot.

Bette Gray

NATIVE SUGAR CAKE

1/2 lb. margarine   1 c. milk
1/2 c. Wesson oil   1/2 tsp. baking powder
3 c. sugar   2 tsp. vanilla
5 eggs   1/2 tsp. salt
3 c. plain flour

Mix and bake at 325 degrees for 1 1/2 hours.
Bette Gray

DATE NUT CAKE

1 c. chopped dates   1/2 c. margarine
1 c. boiling water   1 egg
1 tsp. soda   1 1/2 c. flour
1 c. sugar   1 tsp. vanilla
                              1 tsp. salt

Topping:

1/4 c. margarine   1 c. dark brown sugar

2 Tbsp. sweet milk   1 c. chopped nuts

Combine dates, water and soda, let stand while mixing remaining ingredients. Cream sugar and margarine, then egg and flour alternately with date mixture. Pour into 9 x 12 inch greased and floured pan. Pour topping over immediately.

Pat W. Rollinson

COCONUT CAKE

2 eggs   2 c. sifted flour
1 c. sugar   2 tsp. baking powder
2/3 c. milk   1/2 tsp. vanilla
1/2 c. margarine

Cream margarine and sugar until light in color. Add one egg at a time, beating well after each addition. Sift flour and baking powder and add alternately with milk to butter-sugar mixture. Blend thoroughly. Pour into two greased layer cake pans; bake in moderate oven, 350 degrees, until golden brown and firm to touch. Cool and frost with White Coconut Frosting.

Mrs. Colenda Midgett

OATMEAL CAKE

1 1/2 c. boiling water   1/2 c. sifted flour
1 c. quick-cooking oats   1 tsp. baking soda
1/2 c. margarine or butter   2 eggs, unbeaten
1 c. firmly packed brown   1 tsp. cinnamon
   sugar   1 tsp. nutmeg
1 c. granulated sugar   1/2 tsp. salt

Pour boiling water over oats and mix well. Cream margarine and sugar until light. Beat in eggs. Stir in soaked oatmeal. Sift together all dry ingredients and stir into oatmeal mixture. Turn into a greased 13 x 9 x 2 inch pan and bake at 350 degrees for 30 to 35 minutes. Cool in pan and top with Broiled Frosting.

Mrs. Bethany Gray

MYSTERY MOCHA CAKE

3/4 c. sugar   1/2 c. milk
1 c. sifted flour   1 tsp. vanilla
2 tsp. baking powder   1/2 c. brown sugar
1/8 tsp. salt   1/2 c. sugar
1 sq. unsweetened chocolate   4 Tbsp. cocoa
2 Tbsp. butter   1 c. double strength coffee

Mix and sift together first 4 ingredients. Melt chocolate and butter together over hot water; add to first mixture and blend well. Combine milk and vanilla and add to mixture, stir. Pour into greased pan.

Combine brown sugar, other sugar and cocoa. Sprinkle over top of batter. Pour coffee over whole top. Bake in moderate oven at 350 degrees for 40 minutes. Serve hot or cold with whipped cream. The mystery? It will turn into a fluffy flavorsome cake with a deep pool of luscious mocha sauce!

Bertha Anderson

VANILLA WAFER CAKE

6 eggs	1 tsp. vanilla
2 c. sugar	1 (12 oz.) pkg. vanilla wafers,
1/2 c. milk	crushed
7 oz. coconut	1/2 lb. melted margarine
1 c. chopped pecans	

Beat eggs until foamy, add sugar, vanilla, milk and crushed wafers. Blend. Add margarine and beat, then add coconut and nuts to batter and stir until well mixed. Pour into greased tube pan and bake in moderate oven, 350 degrees, for 1 1/2 hours. Cool and serve.

Mrs. Dorita Ballance

BUSY DAY CAKE

1 pkg. (1 lb. 3 oz.) yellow cake mix	2/3 c. water
	3/4 c. salad oil
1 pkg. (3 oz.) instant lemon pudding	1 tsp. lemon extract
	4 eggs

Glaze:

1 c. confectioners sugar	1/4 c. lemon juice

Mix together all ingredients; beat thoroughly. Turn batter into a 9-inch tube pan. Bake in a 350 degree oven for 30 minutes, reduce heat to 300 degrees and continue to bake another 35 minutes longer.

Glaze: Mix together, spoon glaze over hot cake.

Mrs. P. H. Allen

HATTERAS ISLAND POOR MAN'S CAKE

1 lb. seeded raisins
2 c. sifted flour
1 1/2 c. granulated sugar
2 tsp. cinnamon
2 tsp. nutmeg
2 tsp. allspice

1 tsp. baking soda
1 tsp. salt
1/2 c. melted shortening
2 eggs, well beaten
1/2 c. pureed applesauce

Cover raisins with water and boil for 20 minutes. Sift together dry ingredients, add drained raisins, and stir until well mixed. Mix in raisin water and blend. Add beaten eggs and melted fat and applesauce. Pour into a well greased pan and bake in a moderate oven for 45 to 50 minutes or until cake is firm. Do not use too deep or large a pan, as this cake should be about 2 1/2 inches thick. Serve by itself or cover with a tart lemon sauce. A very old Hatteras Island tradition.

Mrs. Julia Oden

FRUIT CAKE

1 lb. butter
4 c. flour
2/3 c. brandy
1/4 tsp. salt
6 eggs, separated
1 lb. sugar

1 tsp. baking powder
1 lb. broken nuts
2 lb. white raisins
1/3 c. slivered citron
1/3 c. diced orange peel
1/3 c. black molasses

Dredge fruits in 1/2 cup flour, set aside. Cream butter and flour with hands, adding flour a little at a time until well blended. Add baking powder and salt. Beat egg yolks and sugar together until light in color. Beat egg whites until stiff and then fold into egg yolks. Pour into butter-flour mixture, stir well, batter will be very stiff. Add floured fruits and nuts to batter, stir, add brandy and molasses and pour into well greased tube pans. Bake in slow oven, 250 degrees, for 1 1/2 hours. Smaller cakes should be watched carefully after the first hour. Cake should be firm to touch.

Mrs. Colenda Midgett

NUT CAKE

1/2 c. shortening
1 c. sugar
2 eggs
1 1/2 c. sifted flour

2 tsp. baking powder
1/2 c. milk
1 tsp. vanilla
1 c. chopped nut meats

Cream shortening, add half the sugar gradually, cream until fluffy, beat in yolks, one at a time. Sift flour and baking powder; stir in alternately with liquid. Beat egg whites until soft peaks form. Gradually beat in rest of sugar, fold into batter with nuts. Pour into 8 1/2 x 4 1/2 x 2 1/2 inch loaf pan, greased and lined. Bake at 350 degrees about 50 minutes.

CHOCOLATE POUND CAKE

1/2 lb. butter	1/2 tsp. baking powder
1/2 c. shortening	1/2 tsp. salt
3 c. sugar	1/2 c. cocoa
6 eggs, unbeaten	1 c. milk
3 c. sifted cake flour	2 tsp. vanilla

Cream shortening and butter, add sugar gradually, creaming all the while until well blended. Add eggs, one at a time, beating well after each addition. Sift flour and dry ingredients together 3 times. Add to other mixture alternately with milk in which vanilla has been added. Blend thoroughly. Turn into a greased, lightly floured tube pan. Bake at 325 degrees 1 hour and 20 minutes. It is best to have all ingredients at room temperature.

Mrs. Pat Rollinson

COCONUT CAKE SUPREME

4 egg whites, unbeaten	1 1/2 c. sugar
2 3/4 c. sifted flour	1 tsp. vanilla
4 tsp. baking powder	1 tsp. almond extract
3/4 tsp. salt	1 c. milk or coconut milk
3/4 c. butter or Crisco	

Place egg whites in bowl and bring to room temperature. Measure and sift flour, baking powder and salt 3 times. Cream shortening, add sugar gradually and beat well. Beat egg whites until fluffy, add 1/2 cup sugar, beating until whites form stiff peaks. Add flavorings and milk alternately with flour to creamed mixture, blend well. Fold whites into batter and pour into 3 greased round 8-inch layer cake pans. Bake in moderate oven, 350 degrees, for 25 to 30 minutes. Cool and frost with white frosting.

Mrs. Pat Rollinson

POOR MAN'S CAKE

1 lb. (or pkg.) raisins	1 tsp. salt
4 c. all-purpose flour,	1 Tbsp. baking soda
unsifted	1 Tbsp. cinnamon
2 c. sugar	1 Tbsp. nutmeg
1/2 c. margarine, melted	

Boil raisins in 2 cups water 15 minutes, add 1 cup cold water and cool. In large mixing bowl sift together all dry ingredients. With slotted spoon drain raisins from water and mix into dry ingredients until all are well coated with flour, then mix in water in which raisins were cooked. Lastly, stir in melted margarine. Mixture will be thick. Bake in well greased pan, 13 x 9 x 2 inches, at 300 degrees for 40 to 50 minutes, or until toothpick comes out clean. For variations, add chopped nuts, shredded apples or marshmallows (one or all).

Mrs. Cecil L. Midgett

APPLESAUCE CAKE

1/2 c. butter or oleo	1 tsp. baking soda
1 c. sugar	1 tsp. baking powder
1 c. white corn syrup	2 eggs, beaten
2 c. flour	1 c. applesauce
1/2 tsp. salt	1 c. raisins
	1 c. chopped nuts

Preheat oven to 350 degrees. Blend butter, sugar and corn syrup until well mixed. Add dry ingredients and stir well. Add beaten eggs and mix. Stir in applesauce, raisins and nuts, mix and pour into a greased pan. Bake for 45 minutes to 1 hour. Serve either hot or cold.

Mrs. Margaret Midgett

NUT AND RAISIN CAKE

2 c. sugar	1/4 tsp. salt
3 c. flour	1 tsp. vanilla
1/2 tsp. baking soda	1 c. Wesson oil
1 tsp. allspice	3 eggs, beaten
1 tsp. nutmeg	1/2 c. buttermilk
1 tsp. cinnamon	1 c. chopped nuts
	1 c. raisins

Cook raisins in small amount of water until soft. Combine all dry ingredients, add oil, buttermilk and mix well. Add raisins, chopped nuts and vanilla. Stir until well blended. Pour in a greased 13 x 9 x 2 inch pan. Bake in a medium oven, 350 degrees, for about 45 minutes. This cake will cut into 24 servings. Cool cake, leave in pan and cut. Frost with Special Frosting.

Mrs. C. A. Roadcap

BRAZIL NUT CAKE

2 c. ground Brazil nuts
  (pecans may be also
  used instead)

1 c. sugar
1/4 tsp. salt
6 eggs, separated

Grind the nuts and mix with sugar and salt. Beat egg yolks until light and foamy and beat in nut and sugar mixture. Beat thoroughly. Beat egg whites until stiff and gently fold in the nut mixture. Pour into 3 greased 8-inch cake pans and bake in a moderate oven, 350 degrees, for 30 minutes. Or, mixture may be poured into a greased tube pan or spring form and baked in a slow oven, 325 degrees, for 20 minutes and then raise the heat to 375 degrees for 10 minutes; then decrease heat to 325 degrees for 30 minutes. Top with Brazil Frosting.

Mrs. Bounce Anderson

BRAZIL NUT FROSTING

2 egg whites, unbeaten
1 1/2 c. brown sugar,
  firmly packed

1 c. Brazil nuts (pecans may
  be used)
pinch salt
5 Tbsp. water

Put egg whites, sugar, salt and water in top of double boiler. Beat until well mixed. Place over rapidly boiling water, beating constantly with beater and cook for seven minutes, or until frosting will stand in peaks. Remove from fire. Beat until thick enough to spread. Frost cake and decorate with chopped nuts between layers and on top of cake.

Mrs. Bounce Anderson

WHITE COCONUT FROSTING

2 egg whites
8 tsp. sugar

1 tsp. vanilla

Beat egg whites until foamy. Add sugar gradually, beating constantly, until whites peak. Add vanilla and blend. Spread on top and between layers of cake, sprinkle generously with grated coconut.

Mrs. Colenda Midgett

BROILED FROSTING

1/4 c. firmly packed
  brown sugar
1/2 c. granulated sugar
1 c. flaked coconut

1 c. chopped nuts
6 Tbsp. margarine or butter
1/4 c. light cream
1/4 tsp. vanilla

Combine first 6 ingredients. Heat until bubbly. Stir in vanilla. Spread on cake and broil under flame until golden brown, about 5 minutes.

Mrs. Bethany Gray

WHITE FROSTING

2 c. sugar
1 c. water
1/8 tsp. salt
1 tsp. white vinegar

3 egg whites
1/2 tsp. vanilla
1/2 lb. fresh coconut

Combine sugar, water, salt and vinegar in heavy saucepan. Cook over medium heat, stirring constantly until clear. Without stirring, cook until mixture forms a thread when dropped from spoontip, or to 240 degrees. Beat egg whites until stiff. Add hot syrup, beating constantly. Continue to beat until frosting holds shape. Add vanilla and stir. Spread between layers and cover sides and top of cake and then pile high with freshly grated coconut.

Mrs. Pat Rollinson

ORANGE FROSTING

1 Tbsp. margarine
1 c. confectioners sugar
   (sifted)

4 tsp. orange juice
1/2 grated orange rind

Mix all ingredients together and beat until smooth and creamy. Spread with spatula over the top of Orange Saucepan Cookies.

Margarette Lotte

SPECIAL FROSTING

1/2 lb. butter or margarine
1 c. sugar

1/2 c. buttermilk
1/2 tsp. baking soda

Melt butter, add sugar and stir until sugar is dissolved. Keep on low heat. Add buttermilk and soda and stir. Bring to a boil, let cook for about 1 minute, or until frosting is well blended. Pour over cut slices of cake, making sure that frosting goes between the slices.

Mrs. C. A. Roadcap

PINEAPPLE FILLING

1 (#2) can crushed pineapple
2 c. sugar
2 egg yolks
2 Tbsp. cornstarch
2/3 c. milk
2/3 c. water

Strain juice from pineapple. Place drained pineapple and sugar in saucepan and bring to a boil. Mix cornstarch with water. Beat egg yolks until light in color. Stir cornstarch and water into egg yolks and add to pineapple. Cook until thick, stirring constantly. Enough filling for one 3-layer cake.

Mrs. Zenovah Hooper

NUT AND RAISIN FILLING

3 c. raisins
3 c. black walnuts
1 large pkg. white frosting mix

Chop raisins and nuts until fine. Mix frosting following directions on package. When frosting is stiff, blend in the raisins and nuts and spread on top of your favorite white cake. Makes enough filling for between layers on top and sides.

Aldean Hayes

** EXTRA RECIPES **

Pies – Pastries – Desserts

WATER WHIP PIE CRUST

3/4 c. shortening (Crisco, Spry, etc.)	2 c. all-purpose flour
1/4 c. boiling water	1 tsp. salt
	1 Tbsp. milk

Put shortening in a bowl, add boiling water and milk and break up shortening with a fork. Tilt bowl and with rapid cross strokes, whip with fork until mixture is smooth and thick like whipped cream and holds soft peaks when fork is lifted. Sift flour and salt together into shortening mixture. Stir quickly with round the bowl strokes, into a dough that clings together and cleans the bowl. Pick up and work into a smooth dough, shape into a flat round. Place on a sheet of waxed paper, place another sheet of waxed paper on top and roll out to line two 9-inch pie plates. If you desire to use this pastry for a meat pie, substitute boiling concentrated consomme instead of the boiling water. Add 1/2 teaspoon garlic seasoning salt or garlic powder to the sifted flour.

Mrs. L. B. Anderson

PINEAPPLE PIE

1 can (#3) crushed pineapple	2 Tbsp. cornstarch
1 c. sugar	2 egg yolks
1/4 c. butter	

Cook over slow heat. Pour into baked pie crust. Cover with meringue. Bake in 350 degree oven until lightly brown.

Mellie Edwards

CHESS PIE

1/2 c. butter	2 Tbsp. heavy cream
1 c. sugar	1/2 tsp. vanilla
2 eggs, separated	dash salt
1 1/2 tsp. white corn meal	unbaked pie shell

Bake pie shell in hot oven at 450 degrees for 10 minutes, or until baked but not brown. Cream butter, sugar and egg yolks together. Add corn meal which has been stirred into the cream and vanilla. Beat egg whites until stiff, add salt. Fold whites into batter and pour into pie shell. Bake in hot oven, 400 degrees, for 5 minutes. Reduce heat to 350 degrees and bake 10 to 12 minutes longer or until filling is set. If top browns before the filling is set, cover with foil and complete baking. Serve slightly warm. May also be flavored with lemon juice instead of vanilla. This is a recipe that has been in my family for more than 100 years. It is English in its origin.

Mrs. Lansdell Anderson

PECAN PIE

1 c. light brown sugar
1 Tbsp. butter
1 c. white corn syrup
3 eggs, beaten

pinch of salt
1 c. chopped pecans
1 tsp. vanilla
unbaked pie shell

Cream butter and sugar together until light in color. Add well beaten eggs and blend. Add corn syrup, salt, vanilla and nuts and stir all together. Pour into pie shell and bake until firm and browned in a moderate oven, 350 degrees. Serve plain or with whipped cream.

Emma Wright

MY MOTHER'S LEMON PIE

6 eggs
1 1/2 c. light corn syrup
3/4 c. sugar
1 tsp. cornstarch

1/2 c. lemon juice
grated rind of 1 lemon
1 Tbsp. melted butter
1 unbaked pie shell

Meringue:

3 egg whites, room tem-
    perature

1/4 tsp. cream of tartar
3 Tbsp. confectioners sugar

Beat eggs until frothy, add syrup and continue to beat. Mix sugar and cornstarch and add to egg mixture, still beating. Add lemon juice, grated rind and butter. Beat until well mixed. Pour into pie shell. Bake in preheated 375 degree oven for 15 minutes, reduce heat to 300 degrees and bake for 45 minutes longer or until set. Top with meringue.

Meringue: Beat egg whites until frothy, add cream of tartar and continue to beat until stiff. Add sugar, a spoonful at a time, still beating constantly. Put meringue on top of pie, put around edges of pie to make a good seal, and leave surface of meringue rough. Bake for 10 minutes in a 350 degree oven or until just nicely brown. Cool before serving.

Mrs. Lester C. Churchill

VINEGAR PIE

1 c. brown sugar
2 c. water
1 c. vinegar

2 Tbsp. butter
1/2 c. flour
pie pastry

Combine sugar, water and vinegar and bring to a boil. Add butter and stir until it is melted. Mix the flour with small amount of water until smooth and add gradually to the hot liquid, stirring constantly, until mixture thickens. Line a pie plate with pastry, pour in the filling and cover the top of pie with lattice-like strips. Bake in a hot oven, 450 degrees, for 10 minutes, reduce heat to moderate oven, 350 degrees, and bake for 25 minutes. Makes one 9-inch pie.

Mrs. Sudie Payne

BEST EVER LEMON MERINGUE PIE

6 egg yolks, beaten until
  light
1 c. granulated sugar
1 Tbsp. butter
baked pie shell

juice of 2 lemons
rind of 1 lemon
4 egg whites, beaten until
  stiff

Meringue:

2 egg whites

3 Tbsp. sugar

In the top of a double boiler, put the egg yolks, sugar, lemon juice, rind and butter. Cook over hot water just below the boiling point, stirring constantly until mixture is very thick. It must be thicker than ordinary custard, for it should fall and remain in ridges over the surface. Add the hot mixture to the beaten egg whites slowly, beating constantly, then return to the double boiler and cook for a few minutes. Pour this hot mixture into the baked pie shell.

    Meringue: Beat the egg whites until almost stiff, sift sugar over top and finish beating until sugar is blended. Spread over the top of the filling, being sure to make a good seal around the crust edges. Bake in a slow oven, 300 degrees until it is nicely browned on the top of the meringue. Cool and taste the best lemon meringue pie you've ever had!

Mrs. W. T. Plum

LEMON PIE

1 pkg. vanilla wafers
1 can condensed milk
2 eggs, separated

1 1/2 lemons (juice)
2 Tbsp. sugar
pinch of salt
4 Tbsp. sugar

In a pie plate, melt the butter and when melted, coat the tin with it. Line with the whole vanilla wafers, filling in with wafer crumbs. Beat egg yolks with sugar, add the condensed milk and salt, stir. Gradually add the lemon juice until the mixture becomes thick, stir. Pour filling into the pie shell. Beat egg whites until frothy, gradually add the sugar (4 tablespoons) and beat until stiff. Spread over the lemon filling. Bake in pre-heated oven, 400 degrees, until meringue is golden brown.

Mrs. Zenovah Hooper

MINCEMEAT PIE

2 2/3 c. mincemeat   1 unbaked pie shell

Topping:

1 c. sifted all-purpose flour   1/2 c. brown sugar
1/2 c. butter, softened   1/2 c. shredded coconut
                                                     1/2 c. chopped pecans

Pour mincemeat into unbaked pie shell. Place softened butter into flour, blend with fork until mixture is crumbly. Add sugar, coconut and nuts and stir until mixture is well blended. Put evenly on top of mincemeat, spreading topping so all mincemeat is covered. Bake in a moderately hot oven, 400 degrees, until crust around pie is a golden brown.

Mrs. Elizabeth Gray

SWEET POTATO PUDDING

4 large sweet potatoes   2 eggs
1/2 stick margarine   1 1/2 c. flour
2 1/2 c. sugar   1 tsp. baking powder
1 Tbsp. cinnamon   1/2 tsp. baking soda
1 Tbsp. nutmeg   1 c. milk
1 Tbsp. vanilla   1/4 c. margarine
1 Tbsp. lemon flavoring   1/4 c. Crisco
1/4 tsp. salt

Boil sweet potatoes until soft. Peel and place in a bowl, and, using a mixer, blend until mashed. Add the melted margarine, mix well, add the dry ingredients, then the flavorings, eggs, beaten, and the milk. Stir until well mixed. Melt the 1/4 cup of margarine and the 1/4 cup Crisco in the baking pan, pour half of it into the filling and leave the rest in the baking pan. Pour in the filling and bake 1 hour at 350 degrees in a preheated oven.

Mrs. Zenovah Hooper

CHICAMACOMICO POOR MAN'S PUDDING

1 pkg. seedless raisins
3 c. water
3 c. flour
2 c. sugar
1 c. shortening

1 Tbsp. cinnamon
1 Tbsp. nutmeg
1 tsp. baking powder
1/2 tsp. salt

Boil raisins in 2 cups of water for 15 minutes and let cool. Sift together the dry ingredients, add raisins and mix with 1 cup of water. Melt the shortening in a baking pan, pour in the batter with the rest of the shortening mixed in it, into the baking pan and bake for 1 hour in preheated 350 degree oven.

Mrs. Zenovah Hooper

CHICAMACOMICO SWEET POTATO PUDDING

3 to 4 sweet potatoes
4 c. evaporated milk, not
   diluted
1 c. sugar

1 tsp. salt
1/2 stick margarine
1 tsp. vanilla
2 eggs, beaten

Peel and grate into a bowl the sweet potatoes. Add milk, sugar, salt and vanilla. Stir until well blended. Beat the eggs slightly, add to the mixture and beat well. Melt the margarine in the dish intended for the pudding, pour in potato mixture, stirring in the melted fat over the top of the pudding. Bake in 350 degree oven for 40 to 50 minutes or until a knife inserted in the pudding comes out clean.

Mrs. Dalton Hooper

SWEET POTATO DELIGHT

6 sweet potatoes, boiled
   and mashed
1 c. milk
1 c. sugar
1/2 c. raisins

1/2 c. chopped nuts
2 eggs, beaten
1/2 c. coconut
1 Tbsp. melted butter
1/4 c. chopped cherries

Mix all ingredients together until they are well blended. Pour into a casserole, sprinkle with chopped nuts and chopped cherries and bake in moderate oven, 350 degrees, for 20 minutes. If desired, serve with whipped cream.

Mrs. Camille Midgett

LEMON FREEZE

1 c. corn flake crumbs
2 eggs, separated

3 Tbsp. sugar
1/2 Tbsp. grated lemon rind

92

| 1 can Borden's Eagle Brand | 1/4 c. melted butter |
| condensed milk | 1/3 c. bottled lemon juice |

Combine corn flake crumbs with 1 tablespoon of the sugar and melted butter in an 8-inch pie plate or an ice cube tray. Mix well. Remove some of the crumb mixture and reserve. Press the crumb mixture evenly around sides and bottom of dish. Beat egg yolks until thick, combine with condensed milk, add lemon juice and lemon rind and stir until well mixed and thick. Beat egg whites until they are stiff and fold in the 2 tablespoons of sugar. Fold gently into the lemon mixture and pour into dish. Sprinkle top with the reserved crumb mixture and freeze in your refrigerator until firm. Serves 8.

Mrs. Sarah Midgett

SUNDAY DESSERT

1 can Eagle Brand condensed	whipped cream
milk	maraschino cherry
chopped nuts	

Remove end from can and stand in a pot half full of water. Bring water to boil, stirring the milk in the can occasionally. Cook until the milk is a light tan in color. Cool. Place a nice sized portion of the caramelized milk in a bowl, add a dollop of whipped cream, sprinkle a spoonful of chopped nuts over the dessert and top with a maraschino cherry and wait for the delight to appear on faces.

Mr. C. B. Wyman

ORANGE DELIGHT

| 1 large angel food cake | 1 large jar orange marmalade |
| 1 large can frozen orange juice concentrate | |

Pour orange juice concentrate into a pot, do not add water. When orange juice has melted, add orange marmalade and bring just to boiling point, but do not boil. Remove from fire. Place angel food cake in a large bowl, pour over it the orange juice-marmalade mixture, cover with waxed paper and store in refrigerator for 24 hours. When ready to serve, place on serving dish, pour over and around the sauce, decorate with whipped cream and put on top some slivered almonds. A small amount of cointreau may be added to the sauce just before pouring over the cake. This is a good dessert for a hot summer's evening and is very sumptuous to eat.

Berta P. Anderson

PINEAPPLE CUSTARD

2 c. sugar
2 cans milk
2 c. water
6 eggs, well beaten

1 tsp. vanilla
1 large can crushed pineapple
pinch of salt

Beat eggs until light and foamy. Mix milk and water, add sugar and vanilla, pineapple and salt. Stir into egg mixture and pour into greased custard cups or greased pan. Bake in a moderate oven, 350 degrees, until a knife inserted into the custard comes out clean.

Aldean Hayes

** EXTRA RECIPES **

Vegetables, Miscellaneous

BAKED ACORN SQUASH

6 acorn squash	1 Tbsp. brown sugar
1 Tbsp. water	1/4 tsp. ground cloves
2 Tbsp. butter	1/4 tsp. cinnamon
2 Tbsp. light cream	salt and pepper to taste

Halve the squash lengthwise, scrape out the seeds and fiber from the cavity. Put the squash, cut side down, in a baking pan with the water, bake for about 1 hour at 325 degrees, or until tender when tested. When soft, scoop out the pulp from the shells and reserve the shells. Mash the pulp with rest of the ingredients and beat the mixture until smooth and creamy. Pile in the re-served shells, return to baking pan and heat until hot in a 325 degree oven. When ready to serve, place a slice of orange on top.

Bertha P. Anderson

BETTE'S BAKED BEANS

2 cans baked beans (pre-ferably Campbell's)	1 1/2 c. sugar
3 medium onions, diced	6 slices bacon
1 c. catsup	1 tsp. cinnamon

Mix ingredients; place bacon on top of beans. Bake 5 hours at 200 degrees. Serve hot or cold. Serves 10.

Bette Gray

FRESH CORN PUDDING

2 c. corn kernels	1 tsp. sugar
1/4 c. melted butter	3 eggs, separated
1/2 c. light cream	salt and pepper to taste

Beat egg yolks until light and thick. Stir into the corn, melted butter, cream and seasonings. Beat egg whites until stiff and gently fold into the first mixture. Pour into a greased casse-role, place dish in a pan of water and put in a slow oven, 300 degrees, for 1 hour or until pudding is firm. Serve hot.

Miss Emmy Goetze

HARVARD BEETS

3/4 c. sugar	4 c. cooked beets
2 tsp. cornstarch	3 Tbsp. butter
1/3 c. vinegar	1/4 tsp. salt
1/2 c. water	1/8 tsp. pepper

92

Combine sugar and cornstarch, add vinegar and water and boil for 5 minutes. Add beets, sliced, and simmer for 1/2 hour. Add butter, seasonings, stir and serve. Serves 6 to 8.

Mrs. Bethany Gray

TOMATOES IN CREAM

2 lb. firm green tomatoes   1 c. heavy cream
1/2 c. butter   salt and pepper to taste

Halve the tomatoes, sprinkle with salt and pepper. In a large skillet, heat the butter, place the tomatoes in the pan, cut side down. Prick the skins with a fork. Cook over low heat for 5 to 10 minutes, turning once. Stir in cream and cook tomatoes until cream is hot but not boiling. Sprinkle with fresh tarragon and serve with the gravy poured over the tomatoes.

Bertha P. Anderson

FRIED GREEN TOMATOES

6 slices bacon   1. egg, beaten
3 large green tomatoes   bread crumbs
salt and pepper to taste

Fry bacon until crisp. Remove from pan and keep warm. Leave about 2 tablespoons of fat in skillet. Slice tomatoes into thick slices. Dip into beaten egg and then crumbs and fry on one side until brown and turn to other side. Fry until tender. Remove to heated dish. Mix a little flour with the fat left in the skillet, scraping up the brown particles, cook until thick and then add enough water to make a gravy. Pour over the fried tomatoes and top each slice with a piece of bacon.

Mrs. J. F. Weigand, Jr.

PEPPER BAKED TOMATOES

3 tomatoes   1 red pepper, minced
1 green pepper, minced   1 onion, minced
1 c. white sauce   salt and pepper to taste

Halve tomatoes and place in baking pan. Finely mince the pepper and onion, season with salt and pepper to taste and pile a heaping spoonful on top of each tomato. Bake in a moderate oven at 350 degrees 25 to 30 minutes or until vegetables are soft. Serve a helping of white sauce over each tomato.

Mrs. R. L. Hahn

GOLDEN POTATOES

6 boiled potatoes   1/4 yellow corn meal
1 onion, grated   2 Tbsp. hot fat
salt and pepper to taste

Dice into small pieces the potatoes into a bowl containing the onion, seasonings and corn meal. Stir until potatoes are blended with the ingredients. Heat the fat in a skillet until hot enough to fry. Add the potato mixture and cook over moderate heat until brown and crusty, stirring occasionally. Serve hot with fish.

Mrs. J. F. Weigand, Jr.

POTATO PANCAKES

4 large potatoes   1 egg, beaten
1 small onion   2 Tbsp. flour
1/2 c. milk   fat for frying
1 tsp. salt

Peel and grate potatoes and onion into milk, mix with remaining ingredients except for fat. Heat fat and when ready for frying, drop potato mixture by the spoonful into the hot fat. Brown on both sides until crusty and serve with applesauce as a side dish.

Mrs. R. L. Hahn

POTATO DUMPLINGS

1 1/2 c. ready potato flakes   1 Tbsp. minced parsley
1 c. water   3 Tbsp. flour
2 Tbsp. butter   1/2 tsp. salt
2 egg yolks, beaten   1/2 tsp. pepper

Bring water and butter to boil, stir in the potato flakes, salt, pepper and parsley. Mix and beat well. Add the egg yolks and flour and beat until well blended. Have ready a pot of boiling water with a pinch of salt in it. Take up a small amount of potato mixture, roll in some flour to shape into a ball and drop into the boiling water. Do not add too many balls at one time. When done, the dumplings will rise to the top of the water, remove and drain and keep warm until all the mixture is used. They will take about 12 to 15 minutes to cook. Serve with Marinated Pot Roast. You may also brown in melted butter some fine bread crumbs and pour this over the dumplings.

Bertha Anderson

SWEET AND SOUR RED CABBAGE

1 large head red cabbage
3 Tbsp. butter
2 Tbsp. chopped onion
2 apples, peeled and cored
1 tsp. salt

1/4 c. boiling water
1/4 c. vinegar
1/4 c. red wine
1/4 c. brown sugar
1 Tbsp. caraway seed

Discard the outer leaves from cabbage. Cut up into sections, core and shred. Soak in cold water and drain. In a saucepan, saute the onion in butter for 3 minutes, then add cabbage. Cover the pan and simmer 10 minutes. Add apples with the boiling water and salt and caraway seed, stir the cabbage, cover again and simmer over low heat for 30 to 40 minutes or until cabbage is soft and water has absorbed. Add vinegar, wine and sugar and simmer for 10 minutes more. Serve hot, with Marinated Pot Roast and Potato Dumplings.

Bertha Anderson

CORN FRITTERS

2 eggs, well beaten
1 c. corn, fresh or canned
    kernels
1/2 tsp. salt

2 c. flour
1 tsp. baking powder
1/4 tsp. pepper

Beat eggs, add corn, salt and pepper. Sift flour with baking powder and add gradually to corn mixture, making a thick batter, and adding more flour if necessary. Drop by spoonfuls into about 1/2 inch of hot fat, cooking only a few at a time and fry until golden brown on both sides. Drain on absorbent paper.

Mrs. Will Hammel

PATRONIZE MERCHANTS ADVERTISED IN THIS BOOK

Relishes, Jellies, Pickles

CUCUMBER PICKLES

7 lb. cucumbers	water to cover
2 c. lime	

Syrup:

2 qt. vinegar	5 lb. sugar
1 box pickling spice	

Wash and slice into rings the cucumbers. Soak for 24 hours in the lime and enough water to cover. Wash twice in clear water and soak for two hours more. Make syrup, drain cucumbers and put into syrup. Soak for another 12 hours and bring to a boil for 10 minutes. Seal in sterilized jars and cover.

Suggestion: It's better to start at night.

Mrs. Pat Rollinson

OLD FASHIONED PEACH MARMALADE

18 ripe peaches	2 (14 oz.) cans crushed
5 whole oranges	pineapple
granulated sugar	1 c. cherries, pitted and
	quartered

Scald peaches and peel. Put peaches and oranges through coarse blade of food grinder. Measure. Add an equal amount of sugar. Add pineapple. Cook in large kettle until mixture drops from spoon in thick mounds. Add cherries, mix well. Seal in sterilized jars.

Mrs. Bill Thompson

PEACH CHUTNEY

1 large chopped onion	2 Tbsp. chili powder
1 1/2 c. seedless raisins,	1 1/4 lb. brown sugar
chopped	2 Tbsp. white mustard seed
1 clove garlic, chopped	1 Tbsp. salt
4 lb. ripe peaches, finely	1 qt. vinegar
chopped	

In a large kettle, mix all ingredients together. Boil slowly until a deep brown and is slightly thick. Pour into sterilized jars and seal. Makes about 18 pints.

Mrs. H. A. Hahn

PEAR CHUTNEY

7 lb. pears, peeled, cored
   and quartered
3/4 lb. apples, peeled,
   cored and sliced
2 lb. onions, chopped
1 1/2 lb. seedless raisins, chopped

1/2 lb preserved ginger,
   sliced
5 garlic cloves, crushed
1 lemon, juice and rind
1 tsp. salt

Liquid:

8 c. wine vinegar
4 c. brown sugar

8 small hot peppers
8 cloves

Put all ingredients in a large earthenware crock or bowl, let rest while liquid is prepared. In an enamel pan, simmer the liquid ingredients for 5 minutes and then pour over the fruit in the crock and let stand for 12 hours. Transfer to large kettle and simmer for 3 to 4 hours or until chutney is rich and dark. Pour into hot sterilized jars and seal at once. Delicious with cold meats and curry dishes.

Mrs. J. F. Weigand, Jr.

MUSTARD PICKLES

2 qt. green tomatoes
2 qt. small onions
2 qt. string beans
2 heads cauliflower
20 small cucumbers

1 lb. dry mustard
1 Tbsp. turmeric powder
1 gal. vinegar
2 c. sugar
3 Tbsp. salt

Peel, slice tomatoes, slice onions, cut the cauliflower into small pieces, peel and cut into slices cucumbers, string beans should be cut into long slivers. Put all vegetables into a large bowl, and salt vegetables and let stand overnight. In the morning, drain thoroughly. Mix the mustard with the vinegar until smooth, bring to a boil and when a full boil has been reached, add the vegetables, sugar and turmeric. Stir and mix well. Bring to another full rolling boil, let boil gently for 30 to 40 minutes or until vegetables are soft. Pour while hot in hot sterilized jars and seal. Makes about 20 pints.

Mrs. Lina Meyer

SWEET-SOUR SLICED CUCUMBER PICKLES

18 large cucumbers
9 onions
1 1/2 pt. vinegar
1 1/2 c. brown sugar

2 tsp. celery salt
1 1/2 tsp. ground ginger
2 tsp. mustard seed
1 1/2 tsp. pepper

1 1/2 tsp. turmeric powder   1 1/2 tsp. salt
1 1/2 tsp. cinnamon

Peel and slice fine the cucumbers and onions and sprinkle with salt and let stand 1 hour. Drain, add remaining ingredients and put into large kettle; bring to a boil. When a full rolling boil has been reached, remove from fire, pour into hot sterilized jars and seal. Makes 15 pints.

Mrs. Lina Meyer

SPICED GREEN TOMATO RELISH

8 qt. green tomatoes   2 c. minced onions
5 c. vinegar   1/2 c. mustard seed
2 c. minced celery   6 minced red peppers
1/2 c. salt   2 c. sugar

Put tomatoes through meat grinder, also onion, celery and red peppers which have been de-seeded. Add the salt, put into a large bowl and let stand overnight. In the morning, drain the juice until relish is almost dry, add the remaining ingredients; mix and pack into sterilized jars and seal. Makes 12 pints.

Mrs. Lina Meyer

** EXTRA RECIPES **

Index of Recipes

INDEX OF RECIPES

CASSEROLES, ONE DISH MEALS

SOUPS, SALADS

ROLLS - BREADS

MEATS, POULTRY

SEA FOODS

CANDIES, COOKIES

CAKES - FROSTINGS

PIES - PASTRIES - DESSERTS

VEGETABLES, MISCELLANEOUS

RELISHES, JELLIES, PICKLES

ON THE OUTER BANKS

Hatteras Island Motel

RESTAURANT, FISHING PIER
AND
DRIVE-IN

Rodanthe, North Carolina

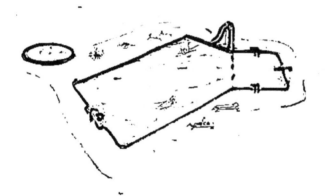

44 ROOMS - EFFICIENCIES - COTTAGES
AIR-CONDITIONED - CENTRAL HEAT
TV LOUNGE - AM FM STERO MUSIC
TWO SWIMMING POOLS - LIFE GUARD

OPEN APRIL 1 — NOVEMBER 30

FOR RESERVATIONS WRITE P.O. BOX 8

CALL 395-2142 AREA CODE 919

About the Author

Tom Kelchner, a native of Pennsylvania, writes about the food and drink of everyday life and their historical background. He blogs at PaFoodLife.com and is the author of *To Great Grandmother's House We Go*, a cookbook and food history book based on the vast archive of 1,400 recipes left by his mother-in-law.

He is a retired journalist, blogger and research analyst. He also is an avid, life-long cook and baker, specializing in dishes of the many ethnic groups who settled in Pennsylvania, including the Pennsylvania Dutch.

He first fell in love with the North Carolina Outer Banks in 1964 on a whimsical Saturday jaunt with several fellow sailors when he was stationed at the U.S. Navy Base at Dam Neck.

He described it:

"It was in October and it rained most of the time we were there. We slept in a station wagon in the parking lot of a grocery market, possibly the one on the Beach Road at Janette's Pier. On the drive down to the Hatteras light house, I remember the amazing beauty and solitude, mile after mile."

"My wife, our dogs and I have been taking off-season vacations to Nags Head for 30 years now. We go in May and October and always stay in efficiencies or rental houses, so I can cook all that fabulous fresh fish."

"The Outer Banks are an amazing place and I hope this facsimile edition helps preserve part of its history."